THE
GOOD
GRIEF
DEVOTIONAL

THE

GOOD
GRIEF
DEVOTIONAL

52 Weeks
toward Hope

Brent D. Christianson

Fortress Press
Minneapolis

A Companion to Good Grief

Cover design: Brad Norr
Interior design: Brad Norr Design
Typesetting: PerfecType, Nashville, TN

Print ISBN: 978-1-5064-5307-1
eBook ISBN: 978-1-5064-5308-8

The paper used in this publication meets the minimum requirements of American National Standard for Information Sciences — Permanence of Paper for Printed Library Materials, ANSI Z329.48-1984.

Manufactured in the U.S.A.

Contents

STAGE NINE: GRADUALLY HOPE COMES THROUGH

STAGE TEN: WE STRUGGLE TO AFFIRM REALITY

Preface

If you have picked up this book, you probably have experience with grief. All people experience grief, of course, but you may be having a more immediate relationship with it in either your own grief or the grief of a friend or family member.

Recognizing the power and difficulty of grief, Granger Westberg wrote a wonderfully helpful book, *Good Grief*, in 1968. Millions of people have found in it validation for their grief, understanding of their feelings, and a way to live through the stages of grieving and into a new reality.

This devotional builds on that work. Following Westberg's ten stages of grief, I have written fifty two meditations, one for each week of the year. My hope is that you will encounter hope in the process of reading, reflecting, praying, and acting on these thoughts.

Grief, of course, is not a smooth and straightforward journey. You may want to look through the table of contents and choose the devotion that most appeals to you at that particular time.

I begin each stage with an introductory reflection on that aspect of grief. Then I consider what that stage means for your self-understanding and your relationships with other people, creation, and God. Each devotion ends with suggestions and questions you can think about and talk about with another person, and actions you might take. Each devotion ends with a short prayer.

I encourage you to honor yourself for the journey you are taking and to always look for signs of hope. All people experience loss and grief. You have chosen to be proactive and productive in your own encounter. May God bless your days and your future.

Brent Christianson
Madison, Wisconsin
Northfield, Minnesota

ONE

When Hope Is Hard

There are times in our lives when we are struck by something so immense and unsettling that we are shocked and find ourselves thinking and behaving in ways we never would have thought we could.

The following poem was written by a person of faith whose sense of self and health and future had been gravely wounded by an unexpected and frightening diagnosis. Wandering through the hymns of his childhood and adulthood, he expresses shock and rage and confusion, questioning his faith and finally crying out to the God who is not shocked by such language and feeling but listens and loves.

Grief

Come thou font of every blessing?
    Come thou, fond of every blessing!
        A maze in Greece How feet are bound
            On Jordan's planes the Baptists fly
      Beautiful Savor,
                Open now the grates of duty
God whose giving knows no sending
        There's no power in the dud

The church's wan foundation
Infirm, the Foundation
Stand up stand up to Jesus
Sigh at Night,   Hold at Night

Night . . .   sight . . .   Sigh . . .
                    Precious
          Lord
Precious Lord . . .
          weak . . . tired . . . worn
Through storm . . . night . . .
cry . . .   call . . .   hand . . .   fall
at   the   river   Home
Home   Home[1]

Shocking? Probably. Not something one might teach Sunday-school students. All people face times when hope seems distant and hardly attainable. The poem is an expression of shock and a feeling of desolation, but notice that it does move to a word of hope and faith. We also can feel that sense of desolation. We have plenty of company there. Our own savior cried, "My God, why have you forsaken me?" (Matthew 27:46). The witnesses to the crucifixion, hearing these words, did not seem to want to believe his grief and chose to think he was calling on Elijah.

We will spend fifty-two weeks considering what grief does to us, how we react to it, and the place of faith—and doubt—in our grief. You will have time to think in the coming days. Close your eyes and consider what you are feeling and doing; think about the world and people around you and how they make you feel. Talk with trusted friends about your experience and your perceptions as you reflect on these devotions. Do you find some meaningful enough to share? Are there some you would like to review and challenge with those friends. Take time to explore the mystery of human life—particularly as, in that mystery, we encounter pain and grief.

To Think About

Have you ever felt the way the poet has?

To Talk About

Most, if not all, people of faith have times when they are angry with God. If you can, speak with a friend about a time you had that experience and how you lived with it.

To Do

Write a poem or meditation expressing your own feelings about times when hope is hard.

Prayer

God, sometimes I find life to be difficult to face. When I am hurting I need your grace and presence. Hold me, God, and see me through the dark days. In Christ, amen.

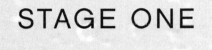

STAGE ONE

We Are in a State of Shock

TWO

To Stand at a Distance

But all his acquaintances, including the women who had
followed him from Galilee, stood at a distance, watching
these things.

—Luke 23:49

I have a very good friend who, years ago, hit a patch of black
ice while driving and slid into an oncoming truck. He was
seriously injured. Months later, when he was describing his
injuries to me, I said, "That must have been incredibly painful." With a bit of a smile, he looked at me and said, "Shock can
be a wonderful thing."

As Granger Westberg wrote, "God has so made us that we can
somehow bear pain and sorrow and even tragedy."[2] He refers to
shock as a temporary anesthesia.

The witnesses to the death of Jesus in the verse from Luke
"stood at a distance." No doubt they were in a state of grief and
shock. Shock is, in a sense, the ability, and maybe the gift, of being
able to stand at a distance when something painful and terrible
has happened.

The experience can be one of overwhelming presence or overwhelming absence.

Mourning Mother in Two Worlds

Sons
Moist maternal air,
full, heavy, everywhere—
neither grasped nor escaped.

No release
but the warm brown river.
Swim beneath a hazy sky

knowing with wisdom
beyond belief
we are water and grief.

Daughters
Empty room,
scent of Sen-sen, smoke,
Mum and perfume,

silence—
no music, echoes,
cries or lullabies.

Close windows
and doors.
No one lives here.

But shock in either circumstance is a state we are allowed, in Westberg's words, as "a temporary escape from reality."[3]

Shock can be a bit like a scab, presented as a sign of hope by John Updike in his poem "Ode to Healing":

> A scab is a beautiful thing—a coin
> the body has minted, with an invisible motto:
> In God We Trust.
> Our body loves us,
> and, even while the spirit drifts dreaming,
> works at mending the damage that we do.[4]

While some helpful forms of meditation ask us to be present to the moment, when something painful happens, when grief attacks us and we feel wounded, it is entirely normal for us to "stand at a distance" and wait, as the companions of Jesus did, for the arrival of hope.

To Think About

What periods of grief have you experienced? Did you experience shock then? If you did, were the periods long or short? Did you experience shock in the same way each time?

To Talk About

Ask others who have experienced grief about their own reactions to their loss.

To Do

Read Granger Westberg's discussion of this stage: "We Are in a State of Shock." Make notes and ask any questions you might have about shock and grief.

Prayer

God of life and death, you were not offended by those who needed to "stand at a distance." Be with me as I also need to keep my distance. But in that distance, grant me grace to know you are with me. Amen.

THREE

When You Don't Feel "Wonderfully Made": Shock and Yourself

Know thyself.

—Ancient Greek aphorism

For I do not understand my own actions. For I do not do what I want, but I do the very thing I hate.

—Romans 7:15

Your primary relationship is with yourself. This may not be your most important relationship—as Christians we confess our most important relationship is with God—but it is your primary relationship. *You* are how you see the world, experience creation, interact with others, interpret events, and live out your day. The psalmist, among other authors in the Bible, marks the wonder of the individual human and writes,

I praise you, for I am fearfully and wonderfully made.
    Wonderful are your works;
that I know very well. (Psalm 139:14)

But sometimes, as in a time of grief and in the tempest of the initial shock, we do not feel "wonderfully" or "fearfully" made, not in any positive way. We may simply see ourselves in our shock and fear or not be able to see ourselves clearly at all.

Self-knowledge is a good and healthy thing, but as even the apostle Paul recognized, it is often illusive even on our best days. In the shock of grief, we don't have a clear vision of the emotional storm that is raging inside us. That lack of clarity can be a burden and make us feel blurry and out of touch. But it is also a gift, because seeing that storm as it rages could do more harm than good at this stage.

What we do feel and see about ourselves at this point is numbness, confusion, emptiness, lack of feeling, lack of focus, lack of energy. The phrase "I'm not myself" rings true while we are in this state of grief.

The song "What Now My Love?" was popular in the mid-twentieth century. Written in French, the English translation of two important lines is:

I now really have nothing to do.
I now really have nothing.

These are words of one who has lost a love, one in a state of grief and, it seems, in a state of shock, one looking at the self and seeing nothing.

Sometimes you experience a dull nothing.

Monotone

Old grey streaked snow
Muted morning clouds
Muffled sound of traffic

Neither cold nor warm
No excitement and no
Agonizing nothingness
Cat still by the window
Not looking for much
Dog rests by the door
A walk would be good
But it doesn't matter
Saturday—weak week
Neither a day of work
Nor a day of worship
No old dishes to wash
No new meals to make
Sit, close your eyes
A dream may come.

These are not comfortable times, but what you are feeling is normal. Granger Westberg notes this in his book; he also notes that in such a circumstance, doing nothing might seem like an attractive option. He suggests that you try to continue your usual activities as much as you can.[1] Sometimes we can think ourselves into a new way of acting, and sometimes we can act ourselves into a new way of thought.

Your relationship with yourself has been wounded. Know that it will heal.

To Think About

Do you have an internal dialogue about your feeling of shock? What are you saying to yourself?

To Talk About

If you know someone who has also experienced a loss, try to connect and have a conversation about your feelings in the early days of the loss.

To Do

Choose one or two elements of your usual daily activities to engage in, adding to the list at least each week.

Prayer

Dear God, I'm not feeling myself just now. I know you know it, but I'm trying hard to understand that too. Help me. Be with me. Let me begin to realize that not only do I share these feelings with all other people but that you know them as well. Be with me, dear God. Amen.

FOUR

If You Want to Talk:
Shock and Others

Now when Jesus heard this [the death of John the Baptist], he withdrew from there in a boat to a deserted place by himself.

—Matthew 14:13a

Hi, Jim,

I'm not sure when the last time was you got a handwritten card, but I have wanted to contact you since Bill's death last week. What a shock that was. He meant so much to you—and to all of us. I just haven't known how to approach you. I don't want to bother you, but I feel bad that I haven't said anything. I'm just not sure what to say. I'm not that religious and I know you are, so I hope that gives you some comfort. If you want to talk, know that I'm available. I'm so grateful for our friendship,

Warmly, Jan

Dear Jan,

Well, I guess you get a handwritten card too! I appreciated getting such a lovely message from you. You are right; I'm very sad and I know others have picked up on that. The fact is, and this may sound harsh—I don't mean it to—but I don't care just now what others are thinking. Someone told me the other day that I'm like the sheepdogs that herders in the mountains of Spain have. When they're wounded, they go off by themselves to heal. I am, as you say "religious," but just now that hasn't healed the pain. Anyway, this won't last. I will be trying to get back into the flow of things. and I appreciate your friendship and patience as I proceed. Thank you very much!

Warmly as well, Jim

When Jesus heard of the violent murder of John the Baptist—his cousin and, in some ways, a mentor—he chose not to be in the company of others. In his sorrow and shock, he left to be by himself.

If you are experiencing the shock of grief, you may also be experiencing that uncertainty about what to do and how to act that Jim and Jan are describing above. C. S. Lewis, in *A Grief Observed*, noted that he thought, as he mourned the death of his wife, that to some of his friends he was "worse than an embarrassment. I am a death's head."[6] Some people may not know what to say or how to act; some may say things that they intend to be helpful, but we don't find them helpful at all. It may be that our reaction is to avoid contact.

When we have friends in such deep grief, we may feel at times that we are being shut out. This may hurt; it may annoy us, or we may understand that our friend or family member needs space—for a time.

When we experience the shock of a grief, we may not feel like ourselves. We may not want to return immediately to our old way of dealing with people in the neighborhood, at work, or in the family. Don't let this frighten or disappoint. We may just need that space—for a time.

Granger Westberg's advice is to make sure this withdrawal doesn't last too long, though. "The sooner the person has to deal with the immediate problems and make decisions again, the better."[7]

Both the griever and the helper are taking deep breaths. When the time out is over and we feel more like being with others, returning to some normal flow of life will feel good.

To Think About

Have you experienced being the griever? Have you experienced being the helper? What do you remember about those times?

To Talk About

If you know somebody who has also experienced "shock"—from physical injuries or from a painful loss, take time to talk with them so you can share with each other what that shock felt like and how it impacted your lives.

To Do

For a griever, begin a list of daily activities you want to continue. For the friend of the griever, let your friend know you are available when they want to talk. Let them know you are available for a walk, a cup of coffee, a shared meal. Seek a time and activity they're comfortable with.

Prayer

God of grief and joy, in Jesus you are no stranger to the grief we face as humans. Help us when we are so hurting that we need to be by ourselves. And help us to return to community. In Jesus's name, amen.

In Bodies So Breakable:
Shock and Creation

When I look at your heavens, the work of your fingers,
    the moon and the stars that you have established;
what are human beings that you are mindful of them,
    mortals that you care for them?

—Psalm 8:3–4

Maybe from the beginning
the issue was how to live
in a world so extravagant

it had a sky,
in bodies so breakable
we had to pray.

—Stephen Dunn, "Ars Poetica"[8]

W e don't just relate to creation; we are a part of it. In grief, and particularly in shock, we experience a brokenness within ourselves—a disjuncture of feeling and thought. So it is really no surprise that we feel that brokenness with other people and with the earth itself.

Shakespeare, who rarely wrote anything insignificant, wrote these words for Hamlet, who was experiencing his own grief and shock:

> I have of late—but wherefore I know not—lost all my mirth, forgone all custom of exercises, and, indeed, it goes so heavily with my disposition that this goodly frame, the Earth, seems to me a sterile promontory; this most excellent canopy, the air—look you, this brave o'erhanging firmament, this majestical roof, fretted with golden fire—why, it appears no other thing to me than a foul and pestilent congregation of vapors. (*Hamlet*, Act 2, Scene 2)

In Hamlet's grief and shock, the earth seems empty and the air is poison. This description of the earth and atmosphere as dangerous and ugly may be extreme, but for those in the shock stage of grief, even the home that is earth and the created order can seem distant, unfriendly, alien.

The biblical witness is different; it sees the wonder and divinity and beauty of the world.

The psalmist reflects something of the awe we humans feel when we look up and around. "For the beauty of the earth, for the wonder of the skies," as the old hymn puts it,[9] reflects something of our "normal" relation to creation. When we suffer a loss, when we are grieving, when that grief shocks us, though, the normal doesn't seem normal. We may not enjoy the same food, the same sounds, the same cities, or the same landscapes we always had. We are, as Westberg wrote, "anesthetized," and, like a person in surgery, we do not see or feel or sense as we do when we are conscious.

In Bodies So Breakable: Shock and Creation

The good news is that consciousness returns. We may be groggy at first, but the familiar becomes once again a place we recognize and welcome. When creation no longer appeals to us or pleases us in this stage, we try not to panic. We try not to fall into the fear that this is how things will always be.

The advice Westberg gives about other relationships also applies to our relationship to creation. We try not to separate ourselves for long from the places, the foods, the scents, the colors, the lands, or the plants and gardens, forests and lakes, mountains and valleys that we have loved and that have given us a sense of connection and comfort.

Whether we are the person in grief or the friend of that person, reconnecting to the natural world will be an important factor in healing. If the weather is good and the body is able, a walk around the neighborhood or through a favorite park or the countryside has the power to restore the connections we have with creation. Closing our eyes to listen and smell helps to focus on what we sense and our own internal reactions. When we open our eyes and see all that surrounds us—both large and small—we find again our place in the world.

Grief is disruption. Disruption is a natural part of life. In its own way, it proves our need for the connections to which we return.

To Think About

What have been some of your most powerful or beautiful or meaningful encounters with the natural world?

To Talk About

Talk with another person about your favorite places you've visited in the world or a place each of you would like to visit.

To Do

Make a definite plan (date and time) to revisit a favorite place, someplace you have found beautiful or meaningful. Add to that list at least, if possible, each week.

Prayer

God, creator of heaven and earth, my own maker, please help me to sense my connection to this world. Give me eyes to see the grandeur as well as the challenges of creation. Give me grace to love my place in the earth. In the name of Jesus, who took flesh to live within creation, amen.

SIX

Draw Near, O Love: Shock and God

Where can I go from your spirit?
    Or where can I flee from your presence?

                         —Psalm 139:7

O God, why are you silent? I cannot hear your voice;
the proud and strong and violent all claim you and rejoice;
you promised you would hold me with tenderness and
    care.
Draw near, O Love, enfold me, and ease the pain I bear.

    —Marty Haugen, "O God, Why Are You Silent?"[10]

The Christian faith proclaims the presence and activity of God to be consistent and clear. But many people have felt themselves witnesses to God's silence, the sense of God's absence or indifference, and have expressed frustration or doubt about God's nearness. That feeling about God is not rare or unusual.

When we grieve and are in the stage of shock, the disruption we experience is not only internal or with people and the world around us. That disruption can also appear in our relationship with God. While our primary relationship might be with ourselves, our most important relationship is with God.

The cry of desertion we may feel echoes the words of Jesus himself on the cross "My God, my God, why have you forsaken me?" (Matthew 27:46). He felt God's silence.

When, in our grief and pain, we question not only the love of God but the very existence of God, those around us may react with their own shock and worry about our souls. What they perceive as our doubt may also summon up uncomfortable feelings for them about their own faith.

We try to keep in mind that if God the Father can put up with such thoughts from God the Son, God can certainly handle our own shocked and challenged faith. I used to tell couples who were preparing to marry to learn how to "fight fairly." I suggested that if there were no disagreements, they might not be taking the relationship seriously.

To bring such doubts, such challenges, such a "fight" to God is not a sign of lack of faith but a sign that we take that relationship with God seriously enough not to be afraid to contend.

When we question God, wonder about God, even doubt God, it is good for us to remember the adage that the opposite of love is not hate but indifference. We are dealing with a relationship of ultimate importance during a highly difficult time in our lives.

We don't give up the dialogue. In this relationship, as with others, it is wise and healthy not to turn our backs on what had been our normal activity.

Have you always prayed or taken time for devotional reading or meditation? Try to continue that practice, but in your prayers, seek to be honest about your thoughts and feelings. God knows them already, but it is good for us to hear ourselves saying those things.

Worship may have always been a part of your life. For some people, it is hard to return to the worshiping community. Returning with a friend or family member often eases the process.

In this stage of grief, things are off kilter. But through all of this, the hope and the promise we have is that when the shock diminishes we will find that God is with us as God has always been, loving us and holding us.

To Think About

Have you experienced other times in your life when God seemed distant or silent? Think about how that felt to you. What words describe that feeling?

To Talk About

Find a good friend, a clergyperson, or a spiritual director and talk about your current relationship with God, your ability to feel God's presence, your desire to feel it, whether you are able to pray or worship. Talk about how your relationship to God feels.

To Do

If worship, prayer, devotional reading, or meditation have been a part of your life but you have stopped those practices, choose one of these activities and set a specific time when you will begin to step back into it. Write it down and note when you have carried it out.

Prayer

God, I'm not sure I want to talk to you now. I need you to help me
know that you have not deserted me, that you hear me, that you
see me, and that you are with me. I think you know how I feel.
Help me to know how you love. Amen.

STAGE TWO

We Express
Emotion

SEVEN

Sighs Too Deep for Words

By the rivers of Babylon—
there we sat down and there we wept
when we remembered Zion.

—Psalm 137:1

When I meet with couples preparing for marriage, I always suggest they develop a "vocabulary of feelings." My experience is that most of us verbally express two emotions—"I'm ticked" or "I'm glad"—and leave all the shades between irritation and exultation alone.

We are wired to be emotional. As Westberg points out in *Good Grief*, this stage is not a call to emotionalism but the recognition that we are creatures who naturally feel and react.

When we are in grief, especially in the early stage of shock, it can be very hard not only to express feelings but even just to feel. We are, for that time, essentially "protected" from feelings that might be overwhelming or potentially harmful when we are reeling from a significant loss or change. But this protection needs to be temporary.

"Emotional release comes at about the time it begins to dawn upon us how dreadful this loss is," Westberg says.[11] As time passes, grief's impact will come more and more to the forefront. When the Israelites were removed from their beloved city of Jerusalem, which was being destroyed, and banished to Babylon, they saw all they held—their self-understanding, community, and faith—torn away like a dry husk. The realization of the depth of their loss came after the shock, and, commanded by their captors to entertain the Babylonians, they instead hung up their instruments and wept. They could do no other.

Feelings are vast and complicated; they often seem out of our control or frightening. But we don't need to be afraid of feelings. We should not fall into the trap of saying some feelings are good and some are bad. They are neither good nor bad, they simply are. The positive or negative comes from what we do with those feelings. The most important thing to do is to express them rather than keep them buried inside. There is nearly universal agreement among psychologists and clergy that what we try to hide is what will control us. When we emerge from the shock of grief, it is not only natural but necessary to express the emotions we have not been able to bring out to the open.

> I buried pain and it came
> up as stalks of anger that
> turned brown and burned as
> flame and turned the world
> around me into "desert"
> that I call "peace."

Sometimes those emotions are a variation on Paul's "sighs too deep for words" (Romans 8:26), and we express our pain in a shriek, a howl, a wordless uttering.

When we are able to express the emotions of grief, we are wise to find another person with whom to share those emotions on an honest and "gut" level. This is where a vocabulary of emotions becomes important. As we share those conversations, we will grow in both understanding and healing.

In the next four weeks, we will explore what the expression of emotions does for our self-understanding and our relationship with others, creation, and God.

To Think About

Are there emotions you have that you tend to find more acceptable and others you find unacceptable? What are they? Why do you think some are more acceptable than others?

To Talk About

Talk with a friend about what you are feeling in your grief and loss.

To Do

Try to expand your own vocabulary of emotions. Think of words that you can use to describe a variety of feelings that you have had. Write an extensive list of emotion words and add to it regularly.

Prayer

Dear God, thank you for the ability to feel. Sometimes I don't want to, I know, but more often I find my own humanity in those emotions. I ask you to help me to be honest with myself and others about my feelings; I ask you to help me be compassionate and understanding with others. In Jesus's name, amen.

EIGHT

Sometimes We Need Yells:
Emotions and Yourself

While I kept silence, my body wasted away
through my groaning all day long.
For day and night your hand was heavy upon me;
my strength was dried up as by the heat of summer.

—Psalm 32:3–4

When we keep our emotions locked up, especially those emotions we may find uncomfortable and hard to deal with or express, we quite often end up feeling like this psalmist: wasting away, groaning inwardly, feeling a heavy hand, and drying up. When we express those locked-up emotions, our minds and our bodies find an entry into healing and hope.

It is not unusual for anger to be our first response to the reality of grief. Lucy van Pelt in *Peanuts* reacts with anger about a situation that grieves her. When her friend Charlie Brown gets sick and then doesn't get better, she storms, "What's wrong with a world where someone like Charlie Brown can get sick, and then not get any better?! I NEED SOMEBODY TO HIT!!" (July 26, 1979). You may find yourself in a similar mood.

Sometimes our anger arises as a response to another feeling. When we find ourselves angry because of our grief, we can try to backtrack to discover what emotion that anger might be a response to—pain, fear, frustration, surprise, confusion at an unfair situation. We will journey into our own souls, our own consciousness, and we will find we know ourselves better than we had before.

When we are able to put not only our finger but a name to the emotion, then we can express it to ourselves. We can talk to ourselves, write to ourselves, meditate on that word and that emotion.

Let the calm hands of grief come.
It's not all as evil as you think.[12]

Being honest about feelings, just as the poet Rolf Jacobsen allows tears and grief to come, is a healing self-expression for us.

Jesus told the parable of the Pharisee and Tax Collector (Luke 18:9–14) who came to pray in the temple. The Pharisee was grateful for how pious he was in comparison to others. The tax collector—a person held in low regard as a thief and traitor—stood at a distance, beat his breast, and asked for mercy. Jesus says, "This man went down to his home justified rather than the other." The tax collector was moved to enter his grief, acknowledge it to himself, and be open about it. And Jesus honored that grief.

C. S. Lewis, in *A Grief Observed*, a journal he kept after his wife's death, spends several pages writing accusations about God that we might not expect from such a person of faith. For example, he questions whether God isn't just a cosmic vivisectionist (someone who likes to dissect living things). The next paragraph begins, "I wrote that last night. It was a yell rather than a thought."[13]

Sometimes we need "yells."

In the next few weeks, we will have the opportunity to consider how expressing emotions has an impact in our relationship with others, with creation, and with God. But the relationship we have with ourselves is as important. An honest expression of emotion—pain, emotional fatigue, sadness, regret, confusion—whichever emotion is a good and healthy way to honor ourselves. We deserve that attention from ourselves. We have experienced a loss, a shock, a cause for grief.

We are allowed and even called by God to see ourselves as people worthy of attention and honesty. As we are able to express grief, to see our humanity in all its height and depth, we find a new and renewed relationship with ourselves.

To Think About

Try to remember times when expressing emotions came easily and times when such expressions were more difficult. What were the emotions? Think about why you found some easy and some difficult to express.

To Talk About

Ask a friend or family member to talk with you about how you each express emotion.

To Do

Write down your primary emotion just now (the moment when you are writing) and then describe it using a color, a shape, a scent, and a picture.

Prayer

God, sometimes I don't know what I am feeling in my heart of hearts, and sometimes I know very well what I feel, and sometimes that frightens me. Help me, you who created me to feel and have emotions, not to be afraid of what I feel, not to try to hide feelings from myself, and not to think faith should be emotionless. In Jesus's name, amen.

NINE

Wounded Healers All:
Emotions and Others

After this Job opened his mouth and cursed the day of his
birth. Job said:
"Let the day perish on which I was born,
    and the night that said,
    'A man-child is conceived.'"

—Job 3:1–3

The book of Job is powerful for many reasons. One thing
it teaches us is how not to react to a friend's expression
of emotion. Job is afflicted in many ways; his friends
come to be with him. They maintain silence until Job
begins his lament, his expression of deep emotions. Rather than
listening to him, they try to correct him, and most of the rest of
the book is Job expressing emotion and his friends increasingly
denying his right to do so.

With grief comes a flood of emotions. When we are able to
put a finger on what the emotions are, we will find great healing
in sharing those emotions with others.

Some people, like Job's friends, will find themselves frightened by our emotions, downplay them, or caution us to suppress or deny what we are feeling. This response may hurt us (and that hurt may lead to anger), so we do need to keep in mind that these people are not cruel. They simply do not know how to honor emotions.

We could feel reluctant ourselves to share honest emotions with others as we move through our grief. C. S. Lewis observed that he was "an embarrassment" to others as he grieved.[14] It is just as likely that he, not so much others, felt embarrassed. If we find ourselves feeling as Lewis did, we don't need to feel bad about ourselves. We are dealing with a flow of emotions that can be confusing and even disorienting.

As we are able to express emotions, however, we may find others who share or have shared similar feelings. We all live in communities—our families, our friends, our neighborhoods, and our work or study life. Some of them will be able to acknowledge what we feel, not rush to assure us that things will get better, and still allow us to express and experience our emotions.

As we are dealing with our own emotions, other people can be a mirror for us, but they are not merely mirrors. They are humans who live life, feel emotions, and are grateful for someone who appreciates their moods just as we value others who acknowledge ours.

We look for others with whom we can be emotionally honest. Family members are some of the people who know us best. They may be the first with whom we can share our feelings, although family members who are grieving the same loss we are facing may have difficulty supporting us because they are attending to their own grief. A few friends also will be available. Sometimes support groups provide opportunities.

What we will find as we move through our own grief and as we are able to share with others what we are feeling is that we are becoming more sensitive to others. We will be more open to hearing the emotional expressions of others. We may even find ourselves being sought out by those who wish to share their own experiences and emotions. We may become, as Henri Nouwen described, a "wounded healer."[15]

As the poet Chana Bloch wrote in her poem "The Potato Eaters,"

> What does a full stomach know
> of an empty stomach?[16]

Emotional openness with ourselves helps us to be more emotionally open and available to other people.

To Think About

As you look back on your life, think about a time someone was emotionally open about themselves with you. How did that make you feel? Pleased they trusted you? A bit frightened by the emotion? Something else?

To Talk About

Talk with others about what friends or counselors or clergypersons they have found valuable when they are sharing emotions.

To Do

Write a letter to someone who has helped you in the past to let them know what their kindness meant and means to you.

Prayer

God, you are busy creating me. You have given me the ability to feel all kinds of emotions. Some of those I greet happily and some of them I want to stay far away from. Help me to feel at home with myself, among my many thoughts and emotions. In Christ, amen.

TEN

Dialogues with the World around Us: Emotions and Creation

[There] may be a grief that's in nature itself. You remember the Latin term, *Lacrimae Rerum*, the tears of things? Men have lived for centuries out there, and they feel that terrific grief of nature and the out of doors and pine trees. There are certain little groves in England, if you walk in there, you'll burst in tears, because there is grief in nature.

—Robert Bly[17]

Poet Robert Bly suggests that there is something deep and holy about the idea that emotion, an aspect of God's creation, is not limited to humans or flesh and blood. We can never be separated from creation. Even in great metropolitan areas, we encounter plants and animals, the sky at night and in the flow of the day. We see the sun, the moon, the stars, and we react to those encounters, those visions.

Our emotions affect how we experience the world around us. The world, creation, will also affect how we experience our grief and our emotional expressions of that grief. If it is true, as Robert Bly states, that there is grief in nature, the notion that even the world can share in our emotions could be a source of some comfort for us.

Sometimes the world we are experiencing fits the emotion we are expressing. The French poet Paul Verlaine, experiencing deep sadness, looked out at his town during a rainstorm and wrote:

> My heart pours out tears
> Like the rain floods this town
> Why must I languish,
> My heart beaten down?[18]

A bright sun might simply increase the hot anger that grief has brought forth in us. A warm afternoon might intensify our fatigue, the emotion of just giving up. A snowstorm can confirm our own feeling of being buried in grief.

There are times when our emotions do not conform to what we see around us. A sunny day might not brighten us, a warm afternoon might not sooth us, the beauty of a snowy field might not calm us when we are expressing deep sadness or anger or a feeling of being disoriented and disowned.

Granger Westberg suggests that some people are embarrassed to express strong emotions out in the open and so may want to find a way to express them more privately. That embarrassment can have different implications for each of us as we relate to creation.

For some of us, the strong emotions we are allowing ourselves to not only feel but to express make it difficult to interact with the outside world, with the creation around us. When this happens, we may simply need space to deal with those strong emotions before we encounter the world around us.

For others of us, a walk in the woods or time in a park or wilderness area where we can let out a cry, a scream, or a stream of tears might be a healthy and healing choice, and frequent outings in the natural world will foster healing.

In these moments of honest and intense emotional expression, it can be wise for some of us not to approach creation alone but to find a friend with whom we can talk about our feelings. It is good to find someone with whom we can take a walk in the woods or in the park. We will be glad to have found a companion who will help us see the life that flows around us even while we are grieving and venting.

Finally, no matter how you initially respond to creation, a dialogue with creation might be helpful. The French Canadian folk song "A La Claire Fontaine" is the account of a man who finds a clear pond and a tall oak under which to rest. A nightingale is singing high up in the tree, and the man tells the bird to sing gaily, since he cannot, because his lover has left him. It could be that this dialogue with creation was healing for him as it could be for us.

To Think About

Think about a time when being out in nature was a positive and healing experience for you. Think about why that was the case.

To Talk About

Talk with a friend about what you both appreciate and don't appreciate about nature.

To Do

Whether your strong emotion matches or doesn't match what you see in creation, write an imaginary dialogue, a conversation with creation about what you are feeling.

Prayer

Gracious God, you created me to live in a world where emotions are real and valuable. Help me to honor those emotions, express them, and not be frightened or ashamed. Hold me in your arms and comfort me. In Christ, amen.

ELEVEN

Being Emotionally Honest
with God:
Emotions and God

I will say to God, Do not condemn me;
    let me know why you contend against me.
Does it seem good to you to oppress,
    to despise the work of your hands
    and favor the schemes of the wicked?
Do you have eyes of flesh?
    Do you see as humans see?
Are your days like the days of mortals,
    or your years like human years,
that you seek out my iniquity
    and search for my sin,
although you know that I am not guilty,
    and there is no one to deliver out of your hand?

                    —Job 10:2–7

Job is angry. As a "secondary emotion," his anger may flow from his pain, thrown off balance by tragedy. He might also be reeling from his friends' insistence that he deserves the tragedy—that God never punishes innocent people.

Job doesn't beat around the bush with his friends or with God. "Oh yeah," Job says, "if that's the case, he's made a big mistake with me." He lets his friends know how upset he is with their simplistic and pious excuses for God, and he lets God know how angry he is with justice that is unjust. In his grief, C. S. Lewis, a man of great faith, also accused God of being a God who "always vivisects."[19]

Sometimes when we face deep grief, especially when others try to assure us that "God doesn't give us anything we can't handle," the emotion we feel about God might be anger. We might also feel disappointment. "You would think a God who had his act together wouldn't kill a healthy twenty-year-old," the father of a university student who died suddenly of a heart attack once said to me.

When we are emotionally honest, we are honest in all directions. That includes our relationship with God.

Of course, such emotional openness does not always lead to us accusing God, holding God responsible for our pain. We may find our relationship with God growing deeper. The Bible includes words of pain and anguish spoken to God by someone who is experiencing pain and anguish. We see such agony expressed in psalms of lamentation.

Turn to me and be gracious to me,
   for I am lonely and afflicted.
Relieve the troubles of my heart,
   and bring me out of my distress.
Consider my affliction and my trouble,
   and forgive all my sins.
Consider how many are my foes,
   and with what violent hatred they hate me.

O guard my life, and deliver me;
  do not let me be put to shame, for I take refuge in you.
—Psalm 25:16–20

There is no need to be at our best when we approach God. God knows the thoughts of our hearts, and addressing what we are feeling to God is both an act of faith and part of the process of self-exploration. When we open ourselves to acknowledge our emotions, God gives us the Spirit that opens our hearts. God is part of that opening.

The Christian faith is an *incarnational* faith. That is, we believe that we see God most clearly in God taking on flesh and blood in Jesus. Jesus showed grief, amazement, fear, joy, and sorrow. When we are open with God in times of intense emotion, we are also open to experiencing God's passion for the world and for us.

A rabbinical story tells of God sitting by the Red Sea after the miraculous escape of the Jewish people from Egypt. God is crying. Moses asks why he is crying and God replies, "I weep for my Egyptian children." God's passion is for the world and for your own grief.

Anne Lamott writes that all essential prayer can be described with the words *help*, *thanks*, and *wow*,[20] all three of which spring from an emotional reaction. As we experience grief, we are unlikely to pray a "thanks" or a "wow" prayer, but "help" prayers proceed from our experience of loss and grief.

To Think About

Were you ever angry with God? When was that, and why did you feel angry?

To Talk About

Talk with another person about emotions you have experienced that you could easily share with God. Talk about emotions you have found you are less able to share with God or pray about.

To Do

Write a letter to God about the emotion you are experiencing and how that makes you feel about God.

Prayer

God, thank you for being open to me as a full human. In Jesus, you experienced and continue to experience human emotions. You honor our human emotions. Be with me when my emotions make me wonder about my relationship with you. Hold me, comfort me, be with me. In Jesus, amen.

STAGE THREE

We Feel Depressed and Lonely

TWELVE

A Necessary Slowing Down

Granger Westberg assures those who grieve, "No two people face even the same kind of loss in the same way. But the awful experience of being utterly depressed and isolated is a universal phenomenon."[21]

Depression is a natural part of human life. In the early days of the human race, if food became scarce, our body's systems would slow down to protect energy availability. In the Global North, such shortages are not common, but we still experience shortages of food, clothing, shelter, and also the loss of a loved one—losses of things that make life livable. Loss, grief, disorientation, uncertainties—all elements of life—can wear us down. A natural response is for our systems to "slow down." This slowing affects our physical strength, our mental and emotional capacities, and our spiritual lives, and we feel depressed.

When we experience a loss that we grieve and the natural slowing that follows, we most likely will feel depressed. While depressed, we find ourselves thinking and behaving in ways that we might otherwise consider not normal. We may not take pleasure in our usual activities or enjoy the company we had previously relished. We may feel worn out and fatigued. We may wonder what God has to do with all this and whether God—or our friends and family—even care.

Feeling Down

Depression
no control
or future

Take a walk?
Say a prayer?
Meditate?

Sip some tea
take a nap
try to dream.

Depression is natural. This slowing down can be a way to recharge, but a long-lasting and deep depression gradually drains us. When we feel that depression, that slowing down, when someone we know and love feels that ongoing depression, we often yearn for someone to be with us, not to offer easy answers but to assure us of love. The presence of someone who loves us and cares for us at a time when we have a hard time loving and caring for ourselves can help us see the positive aspects of our lives.

When we are depressed, often those assurances do not completely burn through the fog through which we see the world, but having a loving companion to walk with us through that fog until it clears makes the journey less frightening.

At the end of the biblical story of Job, God speaks to Job from a whirlwind (Job 38:1), an extreme emptiness surrounded by chaos—the way depression might feel to us. It may seem as though God speaks harshly and angrily to Job. For Job, what's healing isn't so much what God says but the presence of God—who answers, who knows what the emptiness and chaos of grief and depression feel like—that returns Job to life.

When we are depressed, when someone we know and love is depressed, the healing presence of one who will sit with us and be willing to love, even in the middle of what can be a very frightening reality, reflects the presence of God.

To Think About

Think about times in your life when you felt depressed. Who helped you in those times?

To Talk About

If you have a friend or family member with whom you are comfortable discussing depression, talk together about what has been helpful and not so helpful during times of depression.

To Do

Find resources in your community that help people dealing with depression. Make a list of them for yourself or for a friend.

Prayer

Gracious God, open all of us to your grace, that we might know you are present with us when we are happy and when we are sad, when we are moving smoothly through life and when life seems to stand still. Give us faith to doubt and not be afraid. Give us life to move through our fear. In Jesus's name, amen.

Sometimes, a Stranger:
Depression and Yourself

How lonely sits the city
    that once was full of people!
How like a widow she has become,
    she that was great among the nation!
She that was a princess among the provinces
    has become a vassal.
She weeps bitterly in the night,
    with tears on her cheeks;
among all her lovers
    she has no one to comfort her.

                        —Lamentations 1:1–2a

The author of Lamentations writes in response to the destruction of Jerusalem. Israel, never a political power, had been conquered by the great empire of Babylonia and many of its people exiled to Babylon. Jerusalem sits destroyed and lonely, like a widow, like a deserted lover. The poet's words can also describe how we feel when we are depressed and lonely in our grief.

While depression is a slowing or shutting down of some of our internal systems, it can also close us off from ourselves. We become unsure of who we are, what is important to us, what the future holds. We can feel like a stranger even to ourselves.

We can feel lost and alone. The late 1960s/early 1970s rock band Three Dog Night affirmed, "One is the loneliest number." When we are depressed, those tears and that loneliness can have a profound impact on how we see ourselves. We may value ourselves less; we may take less care of our basic daily needs for nutritious food, exercise, adequate sleep, and cleanliness.

As Granger Westberg notes, depression is a normal part of human life, but in our relationship with ourselves we need to remember that depression is not all there is to human life. It is good to acknowledge and face it. We know we are feeling down, we can name some of the valid reasons why we are depressed and not hide from that reality, but it is also good to finally move on.

Depressed on the Solstice

On this, the longest day of the year,
Slow stretch of sunshine, anyway
I am feeling some new pains
And also my old "friend."
The soul has shadows
Not cast by sun
But here, this
Longest
Day.

We are wise not to ignore our depression and our loneliness. All strong emotions, when they are not acknowledged, gain more power over us. But we should also use our own wisdom and the wisdom of our community to help us acknowledge and deal with depression.

One temptation for us is to "self-medicate." Martin Luther, who was often depressed, told his table companions that when the darkness got bad, he drank copiously.[22] Not a good idea, and reading some of Luther's later work, often filled with violent anti-Semitism, sarcasm, and orneriness, one sees the hazards of such self-medication.

Modern medicine does have tools to help deal with a depression that may be too deep or long-lasting. These are helpful resources and, when used under the guidance of a medical professional, can be part of the healing process.

Often, the depression and loneliness are not going to be long-lasting or debilitating, and medication is not necessary. Nevertheless these feelings are painful. It might be good for us to take an "inner journey" to see how these feelings show up most. In physical discomfort? For some people, yes. Some of us experience self-disregard, downplaying who we are and our own gifts. Some simply feel numb.

A special gift to ourselves is to find a trusted friend or guide, one who will acknowledge with us what we are feeling and share in words or simply in sighs and tears what we are feeling and walk with us back to who we are.

We remember these assuring words from the prophet Isaiah:

But now thus says the Lord,
    he who created you, O Jacob,
    he who formed you, O Israel:
Do not fear, for I have redeemed you;
    I have called you by name, you are mine.
—Isaiah 43:1

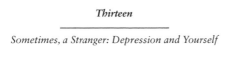

Sometimes, a Stranger: Depression and Yourself

To Think About

Is there a time someone helped you when you felt depressed or lonely? Have you ever helped someone who felt these things? What can you learn from those experiences that might be helpful to you now?

To Talk About

When you are feeling estranged from yourself, talk to another person about what each of you values about the other.

To Do

Write a poem about what you feel like when you are depressed or feeling alone.

Prayer

God, you are with me all through my life. Help me to see myself held safely and lovingly by you and, in that vision, show me how valued and valuable I am. I ask this for Christ's sake, amen.

FOURTEEN

An Invisible Blanket:
Depression and Others

There is a sort of invisible blanket between the world and
me. I find it hard to take in what anyone says. Or perhaps,
hard to want to take it in. It is so uninteresting. Yet I want
the others to be about me. I dread the moments when the
house is empty. If only they would talk to one another
and not to me.

—C. S. Lewis[23]

C. S. Lewis's description of his grief as an "invisible blanket" between him and the world is a fine image for
how we often relate (or don't relate) to others when
we are feeling depressed or lonely. He also reminds us
that loneliness is never the same as being alone. We all need alone
time, but, as Lewis writes, we can be among other people and still
feel lonely.

What is significant for us in Lewis's observation is that while
he felt that blanket between himself and others, he did not hide
from them. For the time being, their presence was not a particular
comfort, but he did not seek to be alone in his loneliness.

When we have suffered a loss and encountered the grief that comes with it, our depression may make us think that nobody really understands us. That is hardly unusual since we can have a hard time understanding ourselves when depression and loneliness set in.

A wise counselor once told me, when I was describing something as "only situational depression," that "all depression is situational!" And it affects the situations we are in. We may find that other people don't seem to feel as deeply as we do. What they talk about and what they do may seem petty and insignificant to us when we are dealing with our own pain. Canadian poet Alden Nowlan, writing about the late Irish activist Bobby Sands, notes that each person can bear only a little of the pain that is not their own.

It may be true, as Nowlan writes, that we are unable to bear much of the pain of another person; at least we can sometimes feel that way. But what will be important for us as we journey through our grief is to continue to be among people. We may not feel the presence of another person to be important for us at the time, but we will find their presence to be welcome and healing.

There is a danger for us, when we seek to be alone in our grief, that this isolation simply builds on itself. We begin to assume, even without thinking of it deeply, that we can "go it alone." When we do that, loneliness simply increases.

Matthew tells us that when Jesus heard of the death of John the Baptist, he withdrew to a lonely place (Matthew 14:13). He needed that alone time to encounter his grief. But soon crowds sought him out, and he moved from loneliness to compassion. We may find ourselves not wanting to deal with others, but as we acknowledge our own grief, our own feelings of depression and loneliness, we also can move into a sense of compassion for others who feel as deeply as we feel. When we heal, we will be able to attend to others in their grief over their own losses—loved ones, homes, situations, finances, health, and other losses we humans can suffer.

To Think About

Remember a time when you felt depressed and lonely. Who helped you through that time?

To Talk About

Talk with a close friend, family member, or clergyperson about strategies for being in community during times of depression. What has worked and what has not worked well?

To Do

Write a list of people you would be comfortable with while facing depression or loneliness. When those times happen, you will know who you can contact.

Prayer

Gracious God, even Jesus knew what it was like to hurt so much it was hard to be around others. Help me to know that even when I hurt so much, Jesus is with me, assuring me of my worth and his love. Help me to reach out to others when I'm down and help me to know that I am meeting Jesus in them. Amen.

FIFTEEN

When the Full Moon Is Hidden: Depression and Creation

In his famous song "I'm So Lonesome I Could Cry," early twentieth century country music singer Hank Williams Sr. looks at the world around him and finds that it reflects his own sadness and grief. A whippoorwill too blue to fly, a moon that hides its face to cry, and a robin weeping all reflect his own grief.

The natural world can reflect our grief. But our grief and depression can also affect how we encounter—and often, how we do not encounter—the world. Just as we can choose to stay away from others while we are feeling depressed, we can let ourselves be shut off from the world around us. Favorite places are no longer favorite. We hole up in our houses rather than taking a walk through our neighborhood, a park, or a forest.

In the Old Testament, the prophet Jonah is on a depressive journey. He has spent some time running from a call from God; when he answers, he does so anticipating that God will destroy a wicked city, Nineveh. When the people of Nineveh repent, God accepts their repentance and Jonah, grieving that he won't be able to enjoy their destruction, becomes depressed. God responds by expressing universal care, love that encompasses all of creation. We are a part of that creation, and our feelings of depression and loneliness, like those of Hank Williams and Jonah, naturally affect the way we see the world around us.

Sometimes, though, what we see in creation gives us the opportunity to express the depression and loneliness we feel.

Full Moon Hidden by Clouds

Passion felt but unspoken,
Perceptions remaining silent,
Problems unacknowledged
Full Moon hidden by clouds.

Talent undernourished
Tenderness kept in check
"Together" prevented
Full Moon hidden by clouds.

Peace unsought
People unnoticed
Patience not tried
Full Moon hidden by clouds.

Faith untested
Freedom not granted
Fantasies not honored
Full Moon hidden by clouds.

Lights left dim
Lives left diminished
Longing left longing
Full Moon hidden by clouds.

These various works—a country song, an Older Testament story, and a poem—witness to the fact that the world around us enables our expression of these bleak moods. At some point, the wonder of the world around us will tell us that we have a partner in the world itself.

The Little Prince, in Antoine de Saint-Exupéry's book of the same name, mentions that on his little asteroid planet he watched the sun set forty-four times in one day because it is good to watch the sunset when one is sad. We may turn to something similar, a place or a setting that soothes when we are depressed or lonely. It could be a place in nature, a theater or museum, a favorite restaurant—anything.

As Granger Westberg notes, depression can seem like a cloudy day; we think the sun has disappeared. Friends might remind us that the sun is still there but, like the moon in the poem, hidden by clouds. We may not "hear" the words of our friends. But eventually the sun will come out.[25]

To Think About

Do you have a favorite place to go when you are feeling down? Think about why that is a good place for you.

To Talk About

Talk with a friend about places that are welcome and healing for each of you.

To Do

When you are feeling depressed, find a place in your world that brings healing to you. If you are unable to physically get there, look for photographs of the place that will boost your imagination.

Prayer

God of all creation, I thank you for placing me in such an amazing world. Sometimes I don't see it as beautiful or amazing, but sometimes you give me vision to find peace in creation. Help me to be in harmony with this world, that we might sing of your love together. Amen.

SIXTEEN

Take My Hand, Precious Lord:
Depression and God

Precious Lord, take my hand,
Lead me on, let me stand,
I am tired, I am weak, I am worn.
Through the storm, through the night,
Lead me on to the light.
Take my hand, precious Lord, lead me home.

—Thomas A. Dorsey[26]

Sometimes we may think that we should go to God the way we go to visit a friend, that is, to make sure we are cleaned up and looking good. But when we find ourselves tired, weak, and worn—the way Dorsey felt when he wrote this song, after his wife and newborn son died—that is when we most need to come to God, just as we are.

In such times we can find ourselves also praying, "Precious Lord . . ." Sometimes that phrase will be an expression of exhaustion as we wonder whether God is present. Sometimes those words will be a plea that God keep God's promises to be with us in times of deep pain.

Does that presence ease the pain and stop the depression and loneliness? Sometimes it does, but there are times when we feel that it doesn't. Well-meaning friends might advise us simply to "turn it over to God" and assure us that things will get better. Still, we might find that "turning over" can be hard to do. And when we are able to move toward God, we don't always feel an improved relationship. We remember that depression puts up an invisible blanket, as C. S. Lewis described it, as something that "comes between." It is there between us and our own self-understanding, our relationships with others, our encounter with creation, and our relationship to God.

It is also important to remember that this blanket, as real as it is, does not block out God. It may feel like that to us at moments of despair, but we are not separated from God. We feel lonely, abandoned, a bit like Jesus in Gethsemane. But we can choose that this sense is not a lasting one. We remember or learn how to pray, we remember or learn how to lament, and we remember and learn how to hope.

We pray to be in conversation with the God who loves us.

We lament because—like Dorsey, like biblical authors, and like Jesus—we know the pain of grief and depression and loneliness.

We hope because the promise we hear—from the Bible, from hymns, from our sisters and brothers—is that God forsakes nothing of what God has made.

The prophet Isaiah, writing to people who thought God had forgotten them, wrote these words:

But Zion said, "The Lord has forsaken me,
  my Lord has forgotten me."
Can a woman forget her nursing child,
  or show no compassion for the child of her womb?

Even these may forget,
  yet I will not forget you.
See, I have inscribed you on the palms of my hands.
—Isaiah 49:14–16

The feelings of depression and loneliness we have after experiencing a loss are real and normal. The God who is with us at those times is real and close as well.

To Think About

Read the words of the hymn that begins this devotion. What thoughts and feelings do you have when you read these words?

To Talk About

With a friend or clergyperson, talk about when and why you sometimes have a hard time believing God is with you in sad times. Talk also about how you experience God in those times.

To Do

Write your own prayer to God about your feelings and what you want from God.

Prayer

Precious Lord, you are always with me. I ask you to help me know that especially in those times of pain and grief and depression and loneliness that I am not alone but that you have promised to be with me forever. Take my hand, Precious Lord. Amen.

STAGE FOUR

We May Experience Physical Symptoms of Distress

SEVENTEEN

I Am Weary with My Crying

Save me, O God,
    for the waters have come up to my neck.
I sink in deep mire
    where there is no foothold;
I have come into deep waters,
    and the flood sweeps over me.
I am weary with my crying;
    my throat is parched.
My eyes grow dim
    with waiting for my God.

—Psalm 69.1–3

The psalmist is not writing about a boating accident; "water" was a universal symbol of chaos. The chaos in the author's life is causing physical and psychological pain. Granger Westberg noticed in his time with people experiencing grief that physical symptoms of distress are common because the mind and the body are never separate. God's love and God's promise are given to us as whole people whose bodies, minds, emotions, experiences, and histories all receive God's grace.

This simply means that when our minds are troubled, it isn't unusual for our bodies to feel signs of trouble as well. We all have experienced upset stomachs when we're anticipating something special or significant—a test in school, a new job, a new home, a marriage. All these, even good things, can stress us and influence our feelings.

What Westberg writes about in this stage of grief is the physical symptoms that may follow a stressful event. Stress and distress can be de-stressed by conversations with friends and helpers and, as the psalmist shows, conversations with God.

Westberg shares an account of the Browns, who move from a small town in Iowa to Chicago for the sake of the husband's promotion. The wife begins to experience physical distress. With the help of a chaplain, she is able to recognize the cause of the illness is her anger, guilt, and grief at the move. Reexamining her life helps her to move into healing.[27]

Grief comes to us in many ways and at many ages. With that grief comes distress and the disruption of our lives.

A student's roommate breaks up with her boyfriend. The student wants to remain friends with her roommate's former boyfriend but feels that would betray her roommate. She is angry at both of them for her dilemma. As a result, she loses sleep and her school work suffers. Her campus pastor explores the situation with her and suggests reframing the situation (give her friends the benefit of the doubt) and talking with them both about her desire to maintain friendships with both of them. The student hears love and forgiveness for herself and for her friends and moves on into the semester with her two friends and renewed strength.

The Christian name for this process of reframing is *repentance*. That doesn't mean only being sorry for sin but reflects the

Hebrew word that means to "turn around" (*shuv*) and the Greek word that means "to have one's mind changed" (*metanoia*).

For Mrs. Brown in *Good Grief*, the physical distress she experienced was certainly not a good thing. None of us enjoy feeling ill! But it became for her, and it can become for us, an inspiration and a reason for looking at our lives, turning around, and having our minds changed as we prepare to move into the future.

To Think About

When has the stress of an event or grief caused you physical distress? When you feel such distress, where in your body does it occur? In your head, your chest, your stomach, your muscles? Try to remember how you were able to feel better when your body has reacted to stress.

To Talk About

Talk with a friend about the experiences each of you may have had following stressful events or times of grief. Have they caused you to rethink aspects of your life? Discuss the changes that rethinking brought about.

To Do

Make a list of those things in your life that you have considered most important to you. Include what used to be important but is no longer as well as things you now find important that you didn't earlier.

Prayer

Gracious God, I thank you that you are always willing to listen to me, always willing to hold me, always willing to comfort me. When I am ill or distressed, help me to keep that good news in my heart. In Jesus's name, amen.

EIGHTEEN

I Just Don't Feel Like Myself:
Your Body and Yourself

So he went and hired himself out to one of the citizens of that country, who sent him to his fields to feed the pigs. He would gladly have filled himself with the pods that the pigs were eating; and no one gave him anything. But when he came to himself he said, "How many of my father's hired hands have bread enough and to spare, but here I am dying of hunger! I will get up and go to my father, and I will say to him, 'Father, I have sinned against heaven and before you; I am no longer worthy to be called your son; treat me like one of your hired hands.'"

—Luke 15:15–19

The prodigal son in this parable demands his share of his father's fortune, runs to a different land, spends all his inheritance, and, when a famine comes, hires himself out as a pig feeder (not a good job for a Jewish man). He is starving. Jesus says, "When he came to himself . . ."

When we are ill, we sometimes tell others, "I just don't feel like myself," and that's because the *self* most of us inhabit is usually well. When grief brings us to a point of physical illness, that feeling of not being ourselves is intensified.

One option, of course, would be to hang on to the feeling, enjoying, in a strange way, the punishment (if we feel guilt) or the chance to have a different kind of pain. That is not an option most people take.

Another option that Granger Westberg proposes is that we take this opportunity to look at what has brought about this illness, if other factors, such as exposure to germs, a flu epidemic, or an accident, don't apply. Often, we can't go through this process on our own. A good friend, a counselor, or a clergyperson might help us reflect on what has been going on in our lives. These people may also have experienced something like what we are going through and may thus be able to give wise counsel, a gift in the midst of our grief.

When we realize that our grief underlies our physical distress, we are moving toward both a greater recognition of our grief and a healing of the distress. We will find that the awareness functions like the clearing of fog or clouds. We are able to see ourselves and others more clearly. A song from the 1960s expresses that new realization:

Johnny Nash wrote:

Gone are the dark clouds that had me blind
It's gonna be a bright (bright), bright (bright) sunshiny day.[28]

We will discover sunshiny days as well. As we explore our own lives and our own grief and become clear about what is important for us as we move forward, we will find that our days, our spirits, and our bodies also clear up. The physical distress that can come about from grief is never a welcome development, but it can be an opportunity for healing and growth.

Ideally, our self-awareness eventually opens the way to positive self-care. Self-care is not selfishness and it is not sinful. Self-care is good stewardship of God's most significant gift to us: ourselves.

Mother Teresa, a saint in her life and a recognized saint of the Catholic Church after her death, cared for the poorest of the poor in Calcutta. Yet, she also cared for herself, her spiritual needs in prayer, mediation, and worship and physical needs by providing the basics she needed for health—lodging, meals, and friendship. That enabled her to be a presence of hope and healing for thousands.

To Think About

Thinking back over your life, do you remember events that were not particularly blessings for you but somehow made you grow? What were they, and how did they add to your growth?

To Talk About

Do you know someone who is good at self-care? Talk to that person about strategies for good self-care.

To Do

Develop a list of activities for your own self-care. Include your emotional and intellectual care (reading? hobbies? relaxation exercises?), your spiritual care (prayer? meditation? devotional and bible reading? worship?), and your physical self-care (exercise? changes in diet? sleep? hygiene?). Make a prioritized list of practices to adopt and follow at least one new activity each week.

Prayer

Generous God, you have created me, and you continue to create me. Thank you for the gift of myself. Please help me to care for myself and help me to honor all other people who are also your creation, your gift. In Jesus's name, amen.

NINETEEN

He Looks Up and Says "Thanks": Your Body and Others

We are created to live in community.

In the early days of the church, there was a hermit known as Simeon Stylites, which means "Simeon who sits on a pillar." He sought to remove himself from the trials and temptations of the earth and lived on top of a pillar for three decades. Was he all alone? No, people had to bring him food and water and do some cleanup. Even if we attempt to withdraw from the world by living on top of a pillar for thirty years, we need others.

Even if we don't *choose* to cut ourselves off from others, though, there are events and circumstances that interfere with our life in community. Illness is one of those things. We all know what it is like to have a common cold and how that impacts how we relate to others. We also know about more serious illnesses that simply knock us out and make us unwilling to interact with others. We get better, and once again enjoy being with others.

When grief makes us physically ill or distressed, it also affects how we relate to other people. It may make us grumpy and ill-tempered. It may drain us of energy, so we just don't feel like being with other people. It may make us resent those who are sound and healthy.

What we seek is to get better and return to community, and the community itself makes this possible.

Taking the initiative to enter and embrace community might be hard for us when we are not feeling like talking to anyone. Encounters will happen, though. They may not be monumental, but they do make a difference.

Visiting a Sick Friend

He rests silent as his dark bedroom
His breathing and the ticking clock
The only sounds that we hear
I read him some stories
He turns and sees me
And when I leave
He looks up
And says
thanks.

Our physical symptoms might not make us bedridden, as the sick friend in this poem is. Still, the community we need may be members of the medical community. It is wise to determine whether our condition is, in fact, primarily medical or the result of grief compromising our health.

We might need other communities, though. We might need trusted counselors or clergypersons who can guide us as we move through a period of reflection, adjustment, and healing. The community certainly will include our friends, people who have known us in a variety of situations. The community we need may be the faith community where we have worshiped and where we have found meaning.

The end we have in mind when we are experiencing this stage is not so much a return to normal, if *normal* means everything is restored to the way it was. Rather, we return to community as persons who have lost something important. We reach out to others, valuable partners in our search, and find healing in community.

To Think About

When has a friend, family member, counselor, or clergyperson helped you through times of bodily distress? What was important to you about their care?

To Talk About

Talk with a friend about how you feel about seeing people when you are ill. How are your experiences and reactions similar, and how are they not similar? What can you learn from one another?

To Do

If you are experiencing physical distress brought on by grief, write the names of four people you would feel comfortable talking to. Contact one or two of them. If you know someone who is experiencing physical distress brought on by grief, contact them and offer to be a listening ear, a quiet presence, or a distraction, or to help with other needs that person may have.

Prayer

God our healer, you have placed all of us in communities. Thank you for my friends and my family, my physician and counselor, and all those who help me. I ask you to give me strength to reach out to them. Give me grace to be a friend. In Jesus's name, amen.

To Rest in the Grace of the World: Your Body and Creation

> Then the Lord God formed man from the dust of the ground, and breathed into his nostrils the breath of life; and the man became a living being. And the Lord God planted a garden in Eden, in the east; and there he put the man whom he had formed. Out of the ground the Lord God made to grow every tree that is pleasant to the sight and good for food.
>
> —Genesis 2:7–9

We have been created to take delight in creation. The Bible's creation stories tell us that we are part of the same earth and the same divine activity as the rest of creation. Creation strengthens us through the food and water it provides, through the recreation and beauty we enjoy in it. We are partners with creation in all that we do with and in our lives.

When we are feeling the physical symptoms of distress, what is intended to delight and strengthen can instead depress and weaken us. Our bodies and minds, both part of creation, seem to

To Rest in the Grace of the World: Your Body and Creation

turn on us. The tasks of being part of creation each day can seem tedious and exhausting. We may look at the world around us not with appreciation but with weariness.

Creation includes nature, food, clothing, neighborhoods, society, our jobs—all that we encounter in our lives. Creation also includes our favorite foods, favorite places, favorite music, hobbies, and ways we relax. But at these times, it may be more important and more healing for us to consider the natural world. Most of us have had experience in the natural world. We may have camped as children or adults. There are probably natural places we have visited and consider favorites—a lake, a seashore, a mountain, or a valley.

We remember what it was like to visit these places and the feelings they gave us. We might have felt relaxed, refreshed, and rested. We might have felt awe. We might have felt curiosity and eager to explore. But most of us have a good memory of a place or places in the natural world.

Wendell Berry, the poet/naturalist, wrote about this in his poem "The Peace of Wild Things."

When despair for the world grows in me
and I wake in the night at the least sound
in fear of what my life and my children's lives may be,
I go and lie down where the wood drake
rests in his beauty on the water, and the great heron feeds.
I come into the peace of wild things
who do not tax their lives with forethought
of grief. I come into the presence of still water.
And I feel above me the day-blind stars
waiting for their light. For a time
I rest in the grace of the world, and am free.[29]

To be able to "rest in the grace of the world," especially when we are feeling physical distress and grief, is a healing gift.

The Japanese have a practice they call *forest bathing*. For many of them, living in populous but heavily forested islands, simply walking through a forest heals the mind and the body. This healing comes from the quiet of the forest, the sounds of nature there. Researchers are also finding the physical properties of the forest—the oils of plants; the scents of earth, foliage, and clean air; the glint of sunlight—have healing qualities.[30]

Creation, including the natural world, is intended to delight and strengthen us. In moments of physical distress, these benefits can be hard to find or appreciate. At these times, it will be good for us to try to move outside—outside both our dwelling places and ourselves. That is, we look outside ourselves for those things that delight, strengthen, and heal. Our time in creation gives us opportunities to reconnect with the world outside that gives beauty and joy to our inner lives.

To Think About

Think about places in your life that you have enjoyed visiting, where you enjoy being. Consider both the natural world and parts of creation that humans have had a part in creating. Why are these places special to you? What do these places have in common?

To Rest in the Grace of the World: Your Body and Creation

To Talk About

Talk with a friend about a favorite place in creation each of you has. Describe your experiences the first time you visited that place. Talk to each other about your feelings then and your feeling now about this place.

To Do

Make a list of no more than five places in creation you have enjoyed in the course of your life. Choose one that is fairly easy to reach and make a plan to visit that place within the next month.

Prayer

God of forest and field, town and country, you never tire of creating and creation. In Jesus you became part of creation, and through him you remind us that your world is holy. Help me, dear God, to see not only the holiness but the beauty and healing around me. Help me to be open to a world that strengthens me. In Christ, amen.

TWENTY-ONE

Touched by God's Own Presence:
Your Body and God

Therefore, since we are justified by faith, we have peace with God through our Lord Jesus Christ, through whom we have obtained access to this grace in which we stand; and we boast in our hope of sharing the glory of God. And not only that, but we also boast in our sufferings, knowing that suffering produces endurance, and endurance produces character, and character produces hope, and hope does not disappoint us, because God's love has been poured into our hearts through the Holy Spirit that has been given to us.

—Romans 5:1–5

I had a track coach in high school who used to quote this passage (in part) when I was running 330s (sprinting three-quarters of the track). "Remember," he would say, "suffering produces endurance." That works for track and other sports, but this sort of pep-talk about the supposed need to suffer in order to get better is not what Paul had in mind.

One of the last things most of us want to hear when we are facing difficulty is the admonition to buck up, take a deep breath, and keep going. The most important aspect of the apostle Paul's teaching about our journey through suffering to hope is the last line of this passage. Hope is possible only because "God's love has been poured into our hearts." This is what we seek to remember when we are experiencing physical distress because of our grief. The bottom line is always the love of God.

It is not always easy for us to keep that in mind. Physical distress is also mental distress, and we may wonder whether the presence and the love of God are real. We may wonder why God isn't healing us at this very moment. Like Job's friends, we may even wonder if God is punishing us for some reason.

At such times, it is good for us to talk with people who will listen to us without seeking "reasons" for our ill health but will simply express their love. It is good for us to have a trusted religious advisor, a friend whose faith and faithfulness we trust, who can speak a word of assurance, or even to have something to read that helps us to know that hope is a gift of God.

Easter Morning

The stone knew before it rolled away.
Touching the earth from which it came,
touching the earth from which all came,
touching the earth to which He came
it felt hope stirring
until promise moved,
surrounded,
and blessed the stone

meant to keep
the living from the dead;
and the stone knew
that life would never part from death
and death would be a part of life
but everything is touched
by God's own presence,
God's own love.
But first, something would happen.
The stone knew . . .

God chooses to be in the shadows of our own physical distress and grief. God is with us to love us into hope.

To Think About

What are you hoping for now? Make a list of your hopes and think about why these particular hopes arise in you. Try to remember other times when you had a particular hope and make notes to yourself about how those times compare to this time.

To Talk About

With a friend, a spiritual counselor, or a clergyperson, talk about what the phrase *the love of God* means to each of you. Talk about how easy or hard it has been for you to believe that God's love is for you.

To Do

Find a concordance of the Bible (a book or online resource that helps you find verses of the Bible containing a particular word or word combination). Look up verses that include the words *God* and *love*. Underline or copy those you find meaningful or helpful. Keep that list for reference.

Prayer

Precious God, you have never been content to keep your love to yourself. You have always poured it out on your creation. Help me to hear and claim your assurance that you pour your love into my heart. When my heart is hurting, I need to know that love. Show it to me, in Jesus, amen.

STAGE FIVE

We May Become Panicky

TWENTY-TWO

Am I Losing My Mind?

Inability to concentrate in time of grief is just as natural as it can be. It would be stranger still if we could easily put aside our grief for routine matters. When something has been terribly important to us for a long time and it is taken from us, we cannot help but be constantly drawn to the lost object. And we suffer daily as we struggle with the gradually dawning realization that it is gone forever.[31]

—Granger E. Westberg

We cannot escape our daily obligations of rising, eating, dressing, cleaning, working or studying, running errands, checking things off our to-do lists, and so on. They are hard to escape, and they are not always pleasant to pursue. When grief is weighing on us and the realization of loss is an ongoing presence in our lives, the daily tasks can become daily grinds.

The distraction of grief, especially if we have always been consistent and careful about our daily tasks, can worry us. Granger Westberg writes that this stage is one of "panic" in that we worry our lack of attention might mean greater problems with our emotional and mental health.

Popular music has plenty of examples of singers worrying about losing their minds, either because something amazing has happened or, more often, because of a lost love. Yes, "losing my mind" may be just a figure of speech, but for people deeply experiencing this stage of grief, the worry, the panic, is real. We may wonder, "What if this is how I'm going to be the rest of my life? Am I losing my mind?"

While we may not choose the word *panic* to describe how we feel—rather, anxious, worried, obsessed—that word portrays an inner scene of turmoil and apprehension about the future.

Those Pedestrian Birds

Those pedestrian birds
whose duty it is to greet the sun,
wake the sleeping: robins, cardinals, a sparrow or two.

    Daily tasks performed
    from habit, not desire,

The tune whistled in the garden,
morning coffee,
regular routines of jog or dog walk.

the walls of the room,
Life itself.

These you note and make notes
to love and honor.

Still, the sun rises,
the heat of the day flattens
your narrow appreciations.

You move, almost intentionally,
   toward evening.

We can often see ourselves moving almost intentionally through the day toward evening, not really aware of ourselves or our tasks. We feel that we are simply doing the motions. Westberg's suggestion is that a healthy thing for us to do in this stage when we feel panic is to "be open to new and different human relationships."[32]

To Think About

When has simply living out daily tasks and responsibilities been hard for you? What was going on at these times? What did you find helpful, and what did you find unhelpful? Why do you find some things helpful? Why do you find some things unhelpful?

To Talk About

Talk with a friend about times when you worried about the future. What were your situations then? How did you feel, and how did you move beyond that worry?

To Do

Write down five events you would like to see happen in the future, whether in days, weeks, months, years, or multiple timeframes.

After some thought, write down one step next to each event that you can take to help make it happen.

Prayer

God, my source of strength and hope, be with me when my own grief and worry weigh me down and the future seems more threat than promise. Bless me with your Spirit and open me to the days ahead. In Jesus's name, amen.

TWENTY-THREE

When We Feel Powerless:
Panic and Yourself

Vanity of vanities, says the Teacher,
    vanity of vanities! All is vanity.
What do people gain from all the toil
    at which they toil under the sun?
A generation goes, and a generation comes,
    but the earth remains forever.
The sun rises and the sun goes down,
    and hurries to the place where it rises.
. . . .
All things are wearisome;
    more than one can express;
the eye is not satisfied with seeing,
    or the ear filled with hearing.
What has been is what will be,
    and what has been done is what will be done;
    there is nothing new under the sun.

               —Ecclesiastes 1:2–9

The author of Ecclesiastes looked at the world around them and looked within and concluded that all is vanity—emptiness and toil. This despair can ring so true when we are moving through grief and begin to panic and worry about ourselves and the future.

In this stage, the future we worry about is one we assume will bear the weight of the loss we are grieving. When we look ahead, it is as though the rear-view mirror blocks our vision, and all we can see is our hearts reviewing the loss and the grief. We have a hard time seeing ourselves doing anything more than passively awaiting whatever is coming at us.

That sense of powerlessness deeply affects how we see ourselves now and in the time ahead. We may be afraid we are obsessing about what has happened. We even may fear, as Granger Westberg notes, that we are losing our minds.[33] In the way that worries have of multiplying, this becomes another source of anxiety and fear about our own experience of panic.

When we have this experience, we keep in mind that, like the whole grieving process, this feeling is entirely normal. We reach a point when we are not quite moving ahead and we are not quite leaving behind what has wounded us. We have stopped the car, pulled to the side, and stared in the rear-view mirror. That disorients us and is a source of anxiety and what Westberg calls *panic*.

Martin Luther, commenting on Ecclesiastes, proposes that anxiety about ourselves is not only wasted effort but is God's business, not ours.[34] This might sound like an admonition not to worry, but Luther intended it as a gospel word of promise and assurance. He is asking us to see that, while our anxiety is real, it is quite often unproductive. God's anxiety about us is productive and ongoing and seeks to comfort and console.

We are entering a new relationship to ourselves in our deepening appreciation of not only the heights but the depths of human experience. We have suffered a loss. All people do, but ours is particular and our own. Grief enables us to enter the shadows it creates.

Our realization that grief can bring about anxiety and panic, while maybe not comfortable, also brings us into a deeper appreciation of who we are, what we feel, and the strength with which we are facing our difficulties. We become aware of what God is healing.

To Think About

Think about times in your life when you have felt particularly anxious about something. What were some of the things that sparked your anxiety? How did you move out of that anxiety? What helped in that movement?

To Talk About

Talk to a counselor or clergyperson about strategies they suggest to deal with an anxiety that goes beyond regular worry. Ask them what resources they have found helpful.

To Do

Following your conversation in "To Talk About," draw up a list of resources and strategies you can turn to when you are feeling anxious. Write them down and keep them in a place you can easily access.

Prayer

Dear God, I can worry about a lot of things. Sometimes that helps me decide to act, but sometimes it paralyzes me. Help me to know that you worry about me too but that your worry for me becomes healing, love, and comfort and life in Jesus. Amen.

TWENTY-FOUR

The Presence of One Who Shares:
Panic and Others

Elijah said to her, "Do not be afraid; go and do as you have said; but first make me a little cake of it and bring it to me, and afterwards make something for yourself and your son. For thus says the Lord the God of Israel: The jar of meal will not be emptied and the jug of oil will not fail until the day that the Lord sends rain on the earth."

—1 Kings 17:13–14

A widow from the city of Zarephath was in deep trouble. Widows were unprotected people at the time, and a famine had reduced what small resources she had to nothing. She was preparing her last supper, a bit of meal and oil. There appeared no future for her. Her form of panic was simply to give up and give in to what seemed inevitable. Who could blame her? Famines have killed millions in human history.

One miracle in this story is the extension of her supply of meal and oil until the famine's end. Another miracle is the presence of one who shares with the widow. The widow and Elijah both gain a new appreciation for the importance of human relationships.

These relationships are not simply about making an acquaintance. They can be the difference between life and death.

When our grief brings us to a place where it is difficult for us to move ahead, difficult even to take care of our daily lives, we could choose, as the widow seems to have chosen, to close shop and fade away. Granger Westberg observes, "We can think of a hundred different reasons why we prefer to stay home and be gloomy rather than go out and be forced to be nice to people and think new thoughts."[35]

The tension we might face is between the desire to avoid being out and about among others and the reality that such interaction will be healing for us. When we are unsure of the future, worried about our own state of mind, we are reluctant to interact with others, perhaps fearing they will sense our uneasy state and be put off.

But Westberg advises, "We must not, however, wallow in our gloom, for it will only prolong our grief work."[36] The reality for us is that we will need the companionship of other people and, as Westberg suggests, be introduced to new and different human relationships. These might be new and different because we will meet new people. But in addition, having experienced grief and worry and dealt honestly with those feelings in ourselves, we will find even longtime relationships will take on a greater depth.

An old Jewish folktale tells of two brothers—one single, one married with a large family—who together farm a field. Each worries about the other—the single brother because his married brother has more mouths to feed, the married brother because his single brother has no children to take care of him when is old.

Every night, each brother secretly brings a sheaf of grain to the other's pile. Each wakes in the morning to find their grain miraculously restored. One evening they run into each other, realize what has been going on, and embrace in joy. Seeing this, Solomon decrees that this place—where humans have met in mutual support and love—will be the site of the temple.[37]

We need the company of other human beings all through our lives, but when we are in a grief that causes worry, panic, and concern about the future, the presence of a brother or sister, like the presence of Elijah with the widow, can be life-giving.

To Think About

Look back over your life and think about people who have been important to you, especially when you have been worried about your future or your own well-being. What has made them important? What words or actions have been healing for you?

To Talk About

Talk with a friend, a trusted counselor, or a clergyperson about concerns you may have about your ability to take care of your daily needs and your fears for the future. Share your thoughts about what might help you deal with those fears.

To Do

Think of someone who has been a helpful and healing presence for you. Write the person a note and thank them for helping you move ahead.

Prayer

God, you have been our help in ages past and you are our hope, you will be my hope, in years to come. Please be with me in those times when I'm not sure of myself, my present life, or my future. Help me to see your love and your joy in me. In Jesus's name, amen.

TWENTY-FIVE

The Promise of the Rainbow:
Panic and Creation

And to the man [God] said,
"Because you have . . .
     . . . eaten of the tree
about which I commanded you,
     'You shall not eat of it,'
cursed is the ground because of you;
     in toil you shall eat of it all the days of your life;
thorns and thistles it shall bring forth for you;
     and you shall eat the plants of the field.
By the sweat of your face
     you shall eat bread
until you return to the ground,
     for out of it you were taken;
you are dust,
     and to dust you shall return."

—Genesis 3:17–19

The account of what is usually referred to as *the fall* in Genesis tells of the brokenness between humans and creation that the biblical authors, and all humans, experience. The faith of Israel proclaimed creation to be good and humankind's role in creation to be one of partnership. The early stories in Genesis seek to explain what went wrong.

When we are grieving to the point of finding our daily tasks and rhythms to be tedious, unappealing, and tiring, when we panic, we feel deeply the brokenness Genesis reveals. Life is toilsome, the ground itself seems cursed, we must battle thorns and thistles that are both literal and figurative. Daily work involves sweat, and all we see ahead is a return to dust.

That is not a particularly pleasant way to live and not a comfortable way to relate to the world.

The biblical authors knew that such a relationship to the world is not rare. We understand that too, and, in the stage of grief that makes both today and tomorrow unclear and unwelcome, we know something of the pain of this brokenness.

New Year

The steep path
moves between oaks
and turns to the right.
Left behind, cold cinders
from last night's fire.
Birds sing past each other
while a stream, beyond sight,
hisses over smooth stones.
Behind an old spruce, stone steps,
worn by age and weather,
descend
into the darkness.

This perception of the world around us is common; it is not abnormal. But it is not a condition we want to remain in.

More often than dealing with the pain and brokenness of human contact with the world, the Bible speaks of our place in it. In the story of Noah (Genesis 6–9), before, during, and after a destructive flood, Noah is asked to care for the world, to rescue other creatures. When the chaos subsides, God assures Noah that God will never again destroy every living creature. God then invites humanity to see that promise in the plants around us and the rainbows above us.

God's rainbow promise tells us that God is no longer interested in retribution but in restoration. We are invited to look again at our world, our day-to-day tasks, and the days that lie ahead with a vision of that restoration and renewal.

Other people will help us move toward this renewal. Family members, spouses, trusted coworkers, those who share our hobbies, those with whom we have experienced the outdoors will be our partners as we once again seek enjoyment in the world around us. We will find, too, that our time and experience in this stage of grief will make us better companions to others and better partners with the world around us.

To Think About

Think about times in your life when your daily work and your experience with the world around you were fulfilling and pleasant. Think about times when they were not pleasing for you. What were the reasons for that difference? What insights do you receive from this comparison?

To Talk About

Who do you know who seems to especially appreciate and enjoy work, chores, and the world around them? Have a conversation with that person about why their perception of and interaction with those experiences is so positive.

To Do

Make a list of daily activities and tasks you enjoy doing (or you used to enjoy doing). Each week, choose one to do and ask yourself what is good about that activity. Write a poem or create a drawing that expresses the goodness you have found in these activities.

Prayer

Dear God, you never tire of your continual work to create and sustain this world—and me. You know sometimes I get tired of the things I need to do to sustain my own daily life and to care for your creation. You know some of them aren't that fun. Give me your grace not only to live in my world but to love my life. Amen.

TWENTY-SIX

A Healing Voice:
Panic and God

So if anyone is in Christ, there is a new creation: everything old has passed away; see, everything has become
new! . . . So we are ambassadors for Christ, since God is
making his appeal through us; we entreat you on behalf
of Christ, be reconciled to God. For our sake he made
him to be sin who knew no sin, so that in him we might
become the righteousness of God.

—2 Corinthians 5:17–21

Dear Mrs. Fielding,

I'm not sure you remember me, but I was in your fifth-grade
Sunday-school class back at Holy Trinity. I think it probably
seemed like I didn't pay much attention to what you were saying and doing. All the boys expected every other boy to act like
we didn't care. But I was really happy to find out that after all
these years, you are still around and you're healthy and you're still
teaching Sunday school!

I hope you don't mind me writing you, but I wanted to reach
out to you. You always seemed so full of, I don't know, faith and

joy and confidence in God's love. I remember you singing "Jesus Loves Me," and, as you warned us, your voice was not so good. But remembering you singing still brings me happiness.

I could use some happiness now. I don't know how much you know about my life after I left town. College, graduate school, meeting Emily, falling in love, getting married, having children. We had the usual ups and downs of married life, and with our son and daughter grown and moved away, we were looking forward to a nice retirement.

I hate cancer. It killed Emily. And, Mrs. Fielding, I'm not sure what I think about God now or whether I can even think about God. I feel something like panic and it scares me. I have trouble concentrating on anything just now, and I don't know if I'm ready to pray or go to church or even talk about faith. Except I guess I'm talking about that now with you.

I remember you telling our class once about a time when you were stuck in your barn during a blizzard. You were very young and very cold and very scared. You said that you knew your dad and mom couldn't come out until the storm stopped and the drifts were taken care of. If I remember right, you said at first you were frantic, running all over, and then you cried a lot, and then as things got dark you wrapped a horse blanket around yourself and felt such great peace.

You said at first you thought you must be dying, and then you realized you would live. You didn't know why you thought that, but you did. You said God spoke to you without words.

I'm waiting for that, Mrs. Fielding. I'm finding it hard to talk to God, but (and I wanted to let you know this) your story and, gee, everything you said and how lovingly you treated us, when

I remember it, for some reason helps me to pray and helps me to try to listen for that God who speaks without words, the one who spoke to you. I'm listening for that God to speak to me.

I remember you talking about being a "new creation," and really, I didn't understand it then; I thought you were arguing against evolution! But when I think about your joy and I stop to think about the God who loves me even when I'm a disobedient fifth grader or a grieving widower, I'm grateful to you for helping me see then and helping me see now how much God loves me and how much I need that love.

Thank you for being God's voice. I even feel better just from writing to you. Write back if you have time. May God continue to bless you . . . and me.

Your child in Christ,

J. J. Petersen

To Think About

Who are the people who have been "God's voice" for you in your life journey? Think about how they spoke and what makes them significant for you.

To Talk About

Talk with a friend about people in your life who have been avenues for you to hear or see or trust God. What did they say or do that gave you clues about God's love? How were they similar, and how were they different?

To Do

Imagine you are Mrs. Fielding. Write a letter back to J. J. and say what you think she would say. Of course, you are using your voice, but see if speaking as somebody else opens you to new ways of seeing yourself and God.

Prayer

Gracious, loving, ever-present God, there are times when life can be overwhelming, and I don't need or want to be overwhelmed by you. I ask you to speak to me in a still, small voice and remind me of how precious I am in your sight. Hear my still, small prayer, my precious God. In Jesus's name, amen.

STAGE SIX

We Feel a Sense of Guilt about the Loss

TWENTY-SEVEN

Create in Me
a Clean Heart

Have mercy on me, O God,
    according to your steadfast love;
according to your abundant mercy
    blot out my transgressions.
Wash me thoroughly from my iniquity,
    and cleanse me from my sin.
For I know my transgressions,
    and my sin is ever before me.
. . . .
Purge me with hyssop, and I shall be clean;
    wash me, and I shall be whiter than snow.
Let me hear joy and gladness;
    let the bones that you have crushed rejoice.
Hide your face from my sins,
    and blot out all my iniquities.
Create in me a clean heart, O God,
    and put a new and right spirit within me.

—Psalm 51:1–8

Guilt can be a very helpful human emotion. "Normal guilt," as Granger Westberg describes it, helps us to realize when we have done something wrong or not done something needed that has hurt someone. Guilt allows us to acknowledge that and seek forgiveness and restitution. Guilt can be a part of any loss.

But Westberg also writes of "neurotic guilt," guilt that has no basis in what we have done but comes from other feelings and may be harder to identify or "forgive."[38]

In the short story "The Story of the Widow's Son,"[39] Irish writer Mary Lavin tells a story with two endings. There is a widow who is making a good living raising and selling chickens. One day, her son is riding home on his bike. He sees his mother's prize hen on the road, swerves to avoid it, and dies in an accident. The widow is stricken with guilt and grief for the rest of her life. Why did she not tell her son he was more important than the hen?

In the second ending, the son does not swerve, hits and kills the hen, and spends the rest of his life in misery and guilt from his mother's scolding. Both stories end with guilt, what Westberg would label "neurotic guilt," that is out of proportion to the reason for the grief.

Lavin's story is a fine lesson in why guilt, whether it is normal or neurotic, needs to be taken care of. Natural guilt is much like the pain of a pulled muscle or broken bone. We have no lasting interest in the pain except for its ability to show us where the wound is. We acknowledge the pain and apply the cure. Neurotic guilt is like an imagined pain. There is no injury, but we still limit our physical activities and our very lives because of what we are imagining as pain or as guilt.

Both kinds of guilt can be debilitating. We seek to deal with them by acknowledging guilt, like the psalmist has done, or, often with the help of a friend or counselor, recognizing that some guilt does not have a sound basis in what we have done or haven't done but requires care as well.

So it will be good for us to consider the place of guilt in our movement through grief, its impact on relationships, and the relief and healing that comes with forgiveness and moving ahead.

To Think About

The character Broadway Danny Rose in the movie of the same name claims guilt is an important human emotion,[40] one without which we would be capable of terrible things. Do you agree? Why or why not?

To Talk About

Talk with a friend about instances of normal guilt and neurotic guilt you have experienced. Remember that the first is the result of something one has done that harms another, and the second is imagined guilt about something that either didn't harm another or didn't happen. It is out of proportion to one's involvement in a situation.

To Do

Find a copy of Mary Lavin's short story and read it. Write down your reactions to what you are reading.

Prayer

Gracious God, you and I both know that your human creations often do not measure up to your expectations. Help all your people to treat each other well and lovingly and help all your people seek forgiveness and restoration when we fail. And help us, when we are feeling guilt for no reason, to look to you for love and gentle honesty about ourselves. In Jesus's name, amen.

TWENTY-EIGHT

We Can't Avoid It:
Guilt and Yourself

Now Peter was sitting outside in the courtyard. A servant-girl came to him and said, "You also were with Jesus the Galilean." But he denied it before all of them, saying, "I do not know what you are talking about." When he went out to the porch, another servant-girl saw him, and she said to the bystanders, "This man was with Jesus of Nazareth." Again he denied it with an oath, "I do not know the man." After a little while the bystanders came up and said to Peter, "Certainly you are also one of them, for your accent betrays you." Then he began to curse, and he swore an oath, "I do not know the man!" At that moment the cock crowed. Then Peter remembered what Jesus had said: "Before the cock crows, you will deny me three times." And he went out and wept bitterly.

—Matthew 26:69–75

What do we do with guilt?

Because we are human, we can't avoid guilt. We all not only make mistakes but do things that hurt other people. Peter had been a loyal follower of Jesus. But when Jesus was arrested and led away, Peter looked after his own safety. He denied even knowing Jesus. The cock crowed and Peter, feeling his guilt, wept bitterly.

What do we do with guilt?

Our response may depend on what kind of guilt we feel, but often we react the same way for both "normal" and "neurotic" guilt.

We might deny we feel any guilt, look for an excuse, or downplay damage we might have done. We might push it down inside us as far as we can. We might blame the other person for putting us in a position where we "had to do" what we did.

When we are dealing with the guilt that is part of the grief process, chances are the person we blame is ourselves. "Why didn't I call an ambulance?!" "How come I didn't learn CPR when I had a chance?" "I should have told him not to drive in the snow!" "Why did I ask her to stop by with all the construction going on?" "Why didn't I visit last summer?" "I sure wish I hadn't told him the story he wrote was stupid." Sometimes the way we deal with guilt is to hate ourselves. This may be the least helpful option—except for refusing to deal with it at all.

We might be feeling regret for something we did or didn't do or say. Such regret is natural, but we experience it as guilt, sorrow for something we did or didn't do that we wish we could change but can't. And that sense of powerlessness is frustrating for us.

Then again, if we are feeling neurotic guilt, guilt that is unrealistic and not based on something wrong or harmful we've done, it can be harder for us to face it. We can let it eat at us (as we can with all guilt) and hope it goes away by itself, or we can just pretend that this is simply the way it is for humans.

Of Course There's Always Guilt

Waiting in the dark
under the last stair,
gray scales, narrow eyes
breath hissing
through yellow teeth,
waiting
there.

The sooner we can deal with our guilt, the healthier we'll be. If we feel guilt for something that is our own fault, the result of our own action or inaction, the best thing for us is to go to the person we believe we hurt. We confess, we apologize, we ask forgiveness. We hope the apology is accepted, but at least we have expressed the guilt and put it "out there." If guilt involves a person whose death we are mourning, it might be healing for us to talk to a friend or family member to express our remorse. A trusted counselor can also help us as we deal with our guilt and move on into our relationships.

To Think About

We all have felt guilt. Think about times in your life when you felt guilty about something you did or said. Focus on just a few times and try to remember both how you felt and how you dealt with it.

To Talk About

Talk with a friend about their own experience of guilt. This doesn't have to be a serious and somber conversation; feel free to express the humor in the situation. But talk together about how you each take care of guilt you have felt.

To Do

If you are feeling guilty about something you said or did that hurt someone, talk to that person, apologize, and ask their forgiveness.

Prayer

Dear gracious and loving God, you are more ready to forgive than we are to acknowledge or confess our sin or guilt. You do indeed forgive. Help me not to be ashamed of guilt but to admit it. Help me not to dwell on guilt but to move on to forgiveness. Help me to forgive myself. Help me to forgive others as well. In Christ, amen.

TWENTY-NINE

We Do Have Options: Guilt and Others

There is no soundness in my flesh
    because of your indignation;
there is no health in my bones
    because of my sin.
For my iniquities have gone over my head;
    they weigh like a burden too heavy for me.
My wounds grow foul and fester
    because of my foolishness;
I am utterly bowed down and prostrate;
    all day long I go around mourning.
. . . .
My friends and companions stand aloof from my affliction,
    and my neighbors stand far off.

                    —Psalm 38:3–11

When our grief moves us into a sense of guilt over what we have done or not done regarding the loss we are experiencing, it affects our relationship with others. The guilt may involve a person or an event, but the guilt impacts our relationships.

We do have options. We may avoid people. Sometimes we blame people. When we come to a good understanding of the reason for our feelings of guilt in our grief, we can move to accept our responsibility for our behavior—and enjoy healing ourselves and our relationships with others.

There is something about guilt that sometimes makes us want to hide. We might try to hide from ourselves in denial or self-hatred. We might try to hide from others, because our guilt has also brought about shame and fear of what fallout disclosure might bring. We worry what others will think if they find out.

We might also choose to blame others for our behavior. My grandson, when he was four years old, specialized in finding someone to blame if something went wrong. Whether he fell off a bike or spilled milk, the problem was that somebody else didn't keep him from doing it.

As we mature, we become a bit more refined in how we go about blaming others. But we still sometimes do it. We might accuse others of not encouraging us to do what is right or not discouraging us from doing what is wrong. We can look at other's faults, assign them greater guilt, and hope that, somehow, we will feel better about ourselves if somebody else is worse.

The author of Psalm 38 is suffering. That suffering could be due to a sense of guilt that is weighing him down. Whatever the reason for his guilt, he is accusing his friends and companions of not being supportive enough.

Both "normal" guilt (guilt from recognizing a wrong we did) and "neurotic" guilt (imagined wrong doing) can lead us either to avoid or blame.

The best option is to accept the fact that something we did or did not do led to hurt. Or we might find that the guilt we are feeling is not necessarily guilt but a deep sense of remorse that can also cloud our world the way guilt can.

As important as making peace with ourselves is the ability to accept others. Our relationships with others will enable us to accept our guilt or accept the fact of imagined guilt, deal with that guilt in positive ways, and move on. As we relate to other people, the exchange of conversation, feelings, thoughts, and questions will help us see our situation more clearly.

Most Christian traditions practice some form of confession and absolution. Martin Luther believed that the value of confessing and then hearing words of forgiveness was not so much that they were necessary for sin and guilt to be forgiven but that hearing another person pronounce complete forgiveness was a healing moment. We look for a confessor, either in a clergyperson or in a trusted friend, who can assure us that guilt is not to be nurtured—that its purpose is to point to what needs to be healed. Acceptance of guilt and the experience of forgiveness brings that healing.

To Think About

Think about times in your life when you felt guilt about something you have said or done or have not said or done. When did you resolve this guilt well? When do you think you could have resolved it better?

To Talk About

Talk with a close friend about times when each of you felt guilty about something in a relationship with another person. Talk about how that felt. Discuss how each of you were able to work through that guilt.

To Do

This may already be your practice, but when you are feeling a sense of guilt, go to a trusted friend or clergyperson. Ask them to hear your "confession" and assure you that you are forgiven.

Prayer

God of deep and lasting grace, there are times when I need to hear and feel your grace. When I am weighed down by guilt, forgive me. Help me to see your ministering grace in the people around me. I ask this in Jesus's name. Amen.

THIRTY

To Blame or to Accept:
Guilt and Creation

Then the eyes of both were opened, and they knew that they were naked; and they sewed fig leaves together and made loincloths for themselves. They heard the sound of the Lord God walking in the garden at the time of the evening breeze, and the man and his wife hid themselves from the presence of the Lord God among the trees of the garden. But the Lord God called to the man, and said to him, "Where are you?" He said, "I heard the sound of you in the garden, and I was afraid, because I was naked; and I hid myself."

—Genesis 3:7–10

M artin Luther, writing about Adam and Eve hiding from God in the garden of Eden, noted that guilt causes us to be "terrified by the rustling of a leaf."[41] When a sense of guilt comes over us and we have not adequately faced it, the earth itself becomes an unfriendly place, a place that can accuse and frighten. As we have noted in our relationship with others, when guilt about a loss is hanging on to us, we sometimes choose to avoid or blame the world, but—ideally—we accept the world as a companion in our journey through grief.

We avoid the world when guilt makes us think that we don't deserve the pleasures that creation offers. We may deprive ourselves of food or drink, activities or places we have found pleasurable in the past. Parks, trips, movie theaters, art museums, a favorite restaurant, or wilderness areas all become less attractive when we are avoiding creation.

We can blame creation itself as well. If our loss was the result of an illness or a natural disaster or an accident, we can sometimes choose to blame the world for our loss and our feelings of guilt. We think, if there were no diseases, if there were no earthquakes, hurricanes, or tornadoes, if street lights and highways were built better, the loss would not have happened. These are responsible for our loss—and our guilt!

Or we can accept that the world, like we ourselves, doesn't always function the way it should. We make mistakes; we sin. Creation, the world around us, contains illnesses as well as cures, bad weather and good weather, poor human constructions and excellent works.

And we can also accept that the world is our partner in God's grace and creation. As we deal with the guilt we feel, it will be important for us not to hide from what had been a delight and not to seek realities we can't fix, just as it will be valuable for us to deal with the loss by helping to find cures for illnesses, protection from disaster, and ways to serve society, volunteering or giving gifts—food, clothing, blood—and to feel like a part of the larger world in our giving.

We probably will find that, along with enjoying conversation with people who can assure us of forgiveness, a good way for us to deal with our feelings of guilt is to take a walk in a park or woods, visit a museum or movie theater, or enjoy a pleasant meal at a favorite restaurant or from our garden or a farmers' market. We return to a creation where we find welcome, acceptance, and forgiveness.

To Think About

What places in the world give you a sense of pleasure and peace? List a few of them and ask yourself what they have in common. If you could not be in or visit those places, would you miss them? Why would you miss them?

To Talk About

Talk with a friend about the places in the world that you have found special. Tell each other what you found special about them. If you have photographs, share them.

To Do

Make a list of five places you would want to go if you are feeling down or have a sense of guilt that could use a change of scenery, someplace to be removed from a daily familiarity that might make you continue to feel down. Keep the list for future reference.

Prayer

Mighty and gentle God of atoms and universes, of all creatures and all that exists, I thank you for your delight in creation. I thank you especially for these places I love so much in the world [*name those you can think of*]. Help me always to find delight in your creation. In Christ, amen.

THIRTY-ONE

Steadfast Love and Mercy:
Guilt and God

Bless the Lord, O my soul,
    and do not forget all his benefits—
who forgives all your iniquity,
    who heals all your diseases,
who redeems your life from the Pit,
    who crowns you with steadfast love and mercy,
who satisfies you with good as long as you live
    so that your youth is renewed like the eagle's.
. . . .
He does not deal with us according to our sins,
    nor repay us according to our iniquities.
For as the heavens are high above the earth,
    so great is his steadfast love toward those who fear
    him;
as far as the east is from the west,
    so far he removes our transgressions from us.

—Psalm 103:2–12

When our loss brings with it a sense of guilt, our relationship with God, like our relationships with others and creation, can take a path of avoidance or accusation or one of acceptance. Last week we read how Adam and Eve, having disobeyed and entered a state God had never intended for us—shame and guilt—hid from God. When we have suffered loss and encountered guilt for that loss, we may try to avoid God, especially if we picture God as someone waiting around the corner to pounce on us for anything we've done wrong. Why would we want to meet the enforcer?

We may also try to avoid God if we're just too embarrassed to be in God's presence. And we may avoid God because we are angry that God didn't intervene in the loss that brings our guilt.

That anger can lead to avoidance, but it can also lead to an accusation against God. "Why should I feel guilty? God, this was all your fault!" This could be our cry, our heartfelt cry. C. S. Lewis, mourning the death of his wife, wrote, "Sooner or later I must face the question in plain language. What reason have we, except our own desperate wishes, to believe that God is, by any standard we can conceive, 'good'?"[42]

Many of us may come to points in our grief journey where we find ourselves avoiding God by avoiding worship, prayer, and devotion. And we may find ourselves accusing God.

As with other aspects of this guilt, the healthy and healing approach we seek is to accept. We accept, yes, the loss and the reality of the guilt—either "normal" or "neurotic"—and in that acceptance, we can deal with it. But even greater is to accept the witness of faith that God forgives completely and freely, removing our brokenness from us "as far as the east is from the west," and that we walk through grief and live in that forgiveness. Such acceptance may not be a matter of simply deciding, "Yes, God forgives," but of being with others who will help us hear that forgiveness and help us, if we have left, to return to worship, prayer, reading, and devotion.

To Think About

When you think about guilt and God, what images come to mind? Do the images include punishment or forgiveness? Think about whether these images have changed during your life.

To Talk About

If you are willing and able, meet with two or three others and discuss how your image of God has remained the same or changed during your lives. Talk specifically about your understanding of the way you think God handles sin and guilt.

To Do

Write a letter to God and speak to God about how you have understood God during your life and what you think about God now.

Prayer

God, my God, our God, God whose will it is to love, I thank you that forgiveness with you is not a reward but a gift. Help me to notice how this gift touches my life. Take my sin and guilt away and let me know you are always with me and I am always with you. In Jesus, amen.

STAGE SEVEN

We Are Filled with Anger and Resentment

THIRTY-TWO

A Gap . . . an Emptiness

For as pressing milk produces curds,
    and pressing the nose produces blood,
    so pressing anger produces strife.

—Proverbs 30:33

Anger is an understandable feeling when we have suffered a loss. We feel a gap, an emptiness. That hollow area in our lives sometimes leaves us with questions about why the loss has happened, and very few answers are completely satisfactory. Anger is a natural response for most of us, but sometimes the anger becomes intense and persistent, a part of our day-to-day experience.

Resentment is a part of human experience as well. Watch little children play. While they mostly will be cooperative and pleasant, we soon find one of the children wants what another has and resents the fact that they don't have it. In grief, resentment can come about as we live through the loss, realizing what has gone for us and what may not be gone for others. We ask ourselves, "Why me and not them?"

Granger Westberg observes, "Even the most devout persons can very well feel angry and resentful, even though we try very hard to sublimate these feelings."[43] The trouble with anger and resentment when they become a prominent part of our grieving is that they are counterproductive. As the writer of Proverbs notes, the concentration of anger produces not resolution or cooperation or an end to anger but strife. Resentment also builds walls and makes enemies and rivals of other people.

Sonnet

We gauge the worth of others and we find
Failure. And we charge our lives to move
Away from those who don't deserve our love;
Apart from those whose status in our mind
Makes them seem a higher, nobler kind,
Whose wealth and grandeur change the way we prove
Our own life's worth. And in that rutted groove
We hide our deepest human needs behind
The shadow of resentment as it jails
Our lives in prisons not unlocked with hands.
The blessing comes when our deception fails
To satisfy our longing and demands
For love. Then Christ appears, and, using nails—
Worded palms, he holds us in his hands.

While anger and resentment are normal human emotions, remaining too long in their control will keep us from moving through the grieving process. Ignoring the fact that they are in us will also inhibit movement to hope.

What we need in this phase is what we have needed all through—supportive and wise human companions who will listen to us express our frustrations and angers and resentments and then guide us through and out of them.

What also can help us in this phase is the world around us. It can be difficult to appreciate the riches of this world, the gifts it gives and the beauty it shares. We live in this abundance. While we are resentful and angry, that may be hard to see, but that creation is healing for us.

As the poem above says, we also need the God who is all too familiar with human anger and resentment and yet does not refuse to be with us when we are feeling resentment for our own pain and anger for the injustice we feel. The human helpers, the bounty of creation and the grace of God will see us through these times when we are taking up emotional arms against ourselves, our friends and families, our world, and our God.

To Think About

When you are angry, where, physically, do you feel the anger—in your chest or your head, your back or your belly, your tightened facial muscles or your clenched fists? Why do you think you feel it there?

To Talk About

When you have worked through anger and resentment—caused by grief or by any other life situation—find a friend to talk to about those instances, what you think caused them, and how you came through them. If you are comfortable doing so, it might be healing for you to talk to that friend while you are still facing these difficult feelings.

To Do

If you have located where anger or resentment seem to touch you physically, try to identify ways to relax those particular places. Practice the exercises while you are not angry or resentful, so when you are, you will have some bodily memory of the letting go. If needed, consult a physical therapist or massage therapist for hints.

Prayer

Dear God, sometimes when I'm angry I scare myself. Sometimes when I'm being resentful I am disappointed in myself. Please be with me in those times and grant me grace and strength to return to myself. In Jesus's name, amen.

Wrestling Our Resentments:
Anger and Yourself

As God's chosen ones, holy and beloved, clothe your-
selves with compassion, kindness, humility, meekness,
and patience.

—Colossians 3:12

The first object of any of our emotions is ourselves. When
we are in a good mood, experiencing emotions that are
affirming and hopeful, we feel better in general. When
we are experiencing emotions that involve blaming
either ourselves or another person or summoning up divisions
between ourselves and others, we feel less well overall.

The Bible, because it is a book about God and humans, contains many examples of people whose pain over loss leads to
resentment and anger. One good example is Saul, Israel's first king.

Young David, a skilled warrior, is a rising star, and the king
is angry and resentful because he has lost status among his people. The first person to be affected by these emotions is Saul,
sitting in his throne room, running through his head all kinds of

schemes to put David in his place. His internal volcano erupts, and he acts violently.

> And the women sang to one another as they made merry,
> "Saul has killed his thousands,
> and David his ten thousands."
> Saul was very angry, for this saying displeased him. . . . So Saul eyed David from that day on. The next day an evil spirit from God rushed upon Saul, and he raved within his house, while David was playing the lyre, as he did day by day. Saul had his spear in his hand; and Saul threw the spear, for he thought, "I will pin David to the wall." But David eluded him twice.
> Saul was afraid of David, because the Lord was with him but had departed from Saul. (1 Samuel 18:7–12)

Because of his jealousy, Saul focuses his anger on David. But the first object of our anger and resentment is often ourselves. We act out this anger and resentment with ourselves by questioning our worth, feeling a tightening of the spirit that anger gives. We aren't sure we want to encounter a world where people and situations make us mad. We may hide.

Anger, while a normal part of the grief process, can also be harmful if we focus it on others. We might direct our anger at a person we think could have helped prevent the loss we are grieving—another driver, a physician, a friend who didn't intervene. We might direct our anger against circumstances that were beyond our control—a loved one's decision to volunteer for the military, a natural disaster, an accident that could have been avoided. We might be angry with God for not living up to what we thought God should be doing.

Our anger could also be free-floating; we might just feel mad without any particular focus. But no matter where we direct these feelings, we ourselves can be the greatest victim of anger. Our internalized feelings can sap our energy and make real encounters with our other emotions more difficult.

As with our anger, we might focus our resentment on others. We might resent a person—someone who survived, friends who seem to be happy when we are anything but happy, someone who has said something that hurt about us, our loss, or a loved one. Our resentment may be against things that don't fit our mood—a sunny day, beautiful music we overhear, the laugher of playing children. We may resent God for God's holiness and nobility when we feel soiled and low.

So, what is important for us, as Granger Westberg notes, is to acknowledge that those feelings are there and then to wrestle with them.

How do we wrestle? Sometimes we are capable of internal dialogue—a conversation inside ourselves about questions such as, "Why am I feeling this? Do I like myself when I'm acting out of anger or resentment? Are there other ways to behave that could help me feel better?"

When we are facing anger and resentment in our grief, we do well to name these feelings, to ask who or what the real objects of our anger and resentment might be, and to continue that wrestling with the help of friends, counselors, and God.

To Think About

Consider times in your life when you have felt either angry or resentful. What were the situations? What were you feeling, physically, at those times? Have you resolved the anger and resentment? If so, how did you do that?

To Talk About

Talk with a close friend about your own experiences with anger you felt was justified and anger that, looking back, you now think was not. Discuss strategies you have used in dealing with your own anger.

To Do

Make a list of five resources that can help you in times of anger or resentment. These can be other people, works of art, poetry, music, or Bible verses. Put the list somewhere where you can find it when you need it.

Prayer

Dear God, I mostly appreciate my emotions, the fact that I can feel and react. But sometimes emotions frighten or bind me. Help me, when I am angry or resentful, to face those feelings, to acknowledge them. Help me, too, to love and value myself as you love and value me. I ask this in Jesus's name, amen.

THIRTY-FOUR

We Don't Need a Scapegoat:
Anger and Others

So when you are offering your gift at the altar, if you remember that your brother or sister has something against you, leave your gift there before the altar and go; first be reconciled to your brother or sister, and then come and offer your gift.

—Matthew 5:23–24

Anger and resentment in our grief process primarily affect us. But we might focus not on ourselves but on other events and people. When we do that, our relationships are negatively affected. Once significant relationships with friends, family members, or coworkers become strained. We may resent those who are happier than we are. Our anger may keep us from seeking out others for conversation.

Holding on to anger and resentment is like making a tight fist. While that fist is tight, we cannot reach out to another, we cannot give anything to or receive anything from another. Eventually, the stress on our muscles—in our hands, up our arms, even into our shoulders, back, and neck—makes us uncomfortable and less willing to interact with others.

Anger and resentment can also have a spillover effect. When we are under the influence of these feelings and focusing on specific people or events, we will tend to distort our relationships. We might see others as if in an amusement park mirror—distorted and unreal. We might easily find things to complain about, whether specific people, ordinary experiences in our own daily lives, or world events.

If you have had this experience, you know that this is not a particularly enjoyable way to live. We can isolate ourselves, ignore friendships, fail to seek advice and counsel.

We may be angry at other people for a valid reason. Someone may have caused an accident. Someone may have supplied drugs or alcohol that lead to a death. Someone may have tried to help and made things worse. Someone may have refused to help, and the grief deepened.

We may have reason to resent others. Some may seem not to share our grief, even though they may be as involved in the loss as we are. Some may have said hurtful things to us, perhaps minimizing our grief or criticizing the person or thing we have lost. Some may have begun a return to normal life and happiness before we did and before we think they should.

Feeling such resentment toward other people can be difficult for us, but the most healing activity we can do is to take steps to restore these relationships. We should first determine whether our anger and resentment are based on actual events. We do that by considering why we are angry or resentful. A trusted friend, counselor, or clergyperson will be a valuable coworker with us in moving through this phase to healing and hope. They can listen to us, help us hear ourselves more accurately, and propose alternatives to anger and resentment.

If we do need to talk with the person from whom we feel estranged, we take a deep breath and contact the person. Sometimes the physical act of a deep breath alone will prepare us. It will also be good to pray for an open spirit as we begin the conversation. If we have a complaint, we try to state it in a way that isn't accusing but focuses on our own feelings. We don't say "you make me angry" but "I'm feeling angry about something you said [or did]." Conversation can clear up your feelings about it and your relationship with that person. It takes work. But holding on to anger and resentment also takes work.

As we deal with the feelings and choose to move forward, we can say:

Someone may have wronged me.

I choose not to wrong myself.

I will forgive them.

To Think About

Consider what things are worth your anger. What things have you been angry about that were not worth your anger? Think about your criteria and reasons for the distinction.

To Talk About

Do you know someone you consider to be particularly good at letting go of anger or grudges and who seems not to become resentful? If so, sit down with them, relate your sense of how they treat anger and resentment, and ask for their advice in dealing with the feelings.

To Do

Has someone hurt or angered you? Think about what you would like to say to this person. Meet with that person after first adopting a willingness to forgive.

Prayer

Gracious God, thank you for placing me in a larger community of people. I really love many of them. Thank you for them. Some of them get me angry. And I'm angry at some for no good reason. Give me your Spirit. Clear my heart and mind and help me seek reconciliation and a restored relationship with my brothers and sisters. In Jesus's name, amen.

THIRTY-FIVE

The Ability to Say Goodbye:
Anger and Creation

The wise have eyes in their head,
  but fools walk in darkness.
Yet I perceived that the same fate befalls all of them. Then
I said to myself, "What happens to the fool will happen to
me also; why then have I been so very wise?" And I said
to myself that this also is vanity. . . . I hated all my toil in
which I had toiled under the sun, seeing that I must leave
it to those who come after me—and who knows whether
they will be wise or foolish? Yet they will be master of all
for which I toiled and used my wisdom under the sun.
This also is vanity.

—Ecclesiastes 2:14–19

The author of Ecclesiastes is complaining, covering almost
the whole gambit of human experience—from hope to
despair, from wealth to poverty, from life to death, from
meaning to meaninglessness. In these verses, he is looking with what sure sounds like anger and resentment at the way
the world, in his eyes, tends to operate. He sees vanity—wasted
effort, tedious toil, and disappointment.

When our grief is leading us to anger and resentment, the world no longer seems like home. We spend so much of our energy on the anger and resentment that paying attention to creation—our work and callings, the outside world, the parks and woodlands and lakes and streams, daytime and nighttime, the earth and the sky, friends and family, food and drink—is difficult and sometimes feels impossible.

Remember, the one most affected by anger and resentment is the one who is angry and resentful. Just as anger and resentment are natural parts of the grieving process, so are the resulting fatigue and indifference to the world around us. Anger and resentment wear us down, eating away at our energy and our capacity to attend to creation.

Some of our anger is understandable. If we are mourning a death from disease, we can be angry with a world where diseases take loved ones away. If we are mourning a loss due to a natural disaster, we can be angry with a world where tornadoes, floods, earthquakes, or hurricanes happen, even though our anger will not change the course of nature. We can be angry at an economic system that often makes obtaining health care difficult or seems to have too much influence on where and how we live.

We might be resentful of a world, as we noted a couple weeks ago, where the weather does not reflect our moods, where we must endure sunny days and happy birds when we feel neither sunny nor happy. Feeling anger and resentment at this world is understandable.

We might also be angry that the world, as the author of Ecclesiastes expresses, is not always agreeable or easy to move through, that it includes sickness, disagreements, and endings. But the peaceable kingdom has never existed, and such anger and resentment are not reasonable.

Still, experiencing the reality and challenges of change, of shared life, and even of our own wearing out can make us wiser and more sensitive to the needs of others.

The Comfort of Old Clothes

The more they faded,
The better they felt.
A hole in the knees fixed
With an iron-on patch.
You change into them to relax.

Eventually the jeans became
Cut-off shorts; you could even
Braid the cotton strands.
Beaten by time but full of memories,
Finally snuck into the trash by mom.

We learned through our clothes
The value of getting-to-know,
The dearness of shared life,
The many ways to adjust,
The ability to say "good bye."

We grow as we move through the grief of losing something or someone that had made life good and comfortable and loving. We grow as we confront our shock, anger, and resentment at having these taken away. We grow as we move through our grief, and we feel more at home in this world.

To Think About

Have there been times when you looked at the world around you and found yourself angry, resentful, disinterested, or disgusted by the world? What brought about this reaction in you? How was that situation resolved for you? Did you resolve it alone or with the help of others?

To Talk About

If someone who is sharing your particular loss is nearby and you feel comfortable doing so, invite that person to join you somewhere outside. It could be a park, a wilderness area, or on the sidewalk or road outside your home. Talk to each other about what you are seeing and whether and how your grief is influencing what and how you see.

To Do

If you are in the stage of anger and resentment, try to find a place to sit outside, preferably in a quiet spot. Write down a word or phrase that reflects some of what you're feeling. Sit down, close your eyes, take a couple deep cleansing breaths, open your eyes, and, focusing on one aspect of or object in your environment for ten minutes, repeat the phrase or word you wrote down. When you are done, close your eyes, take a couple cleansing breaths, and write next to your phrase a different word or phrase that came to you as you meditated.

Prayer

Dear God, help me to be still and know you are God. Amen.

THIRTY-SIX

Disappointed?
Anger and God

O Lord, you have enticed me,
    and I was enticed;
you have overpowered me,
    and you have prevailed.
I have become a laughingstock all day long;
    everyone mocks me.
For the word of the Lord has become for me
    a reproach and derision all day long.
. . . .
Cursed be the day
    on which I was born!
The day when my mother bore me,
    let it not be blessed!

—Jeremiah 20:7–14

The prophet Jeremiah was angry and resentful. He had felt the compelling call from God to prophesy against the sins of Judah and Jerusalem. The result for Jeremiah was that he was persecuted and rejected, mocked and imprisoned. Several times he takes his complaints to God, and in the text above he accuses God of playing unfairly, of being a kind of bully. Yet Jeremiah continues to serve as a prophet.

The impact of our anger and resentment as we mourn touches us. Because our relationship with God is our primary one, anger and resentment are also reflected there. Granger Westberg observes, "One day we may say, 'Why did God do this to me?' or 'How can he be a God of love if he treats people like this?' With Thomas Carlyle we cynically say, 'God sits in his heaven and does nothing.'"[44]

At the death of his wife, C. S. Lewis was disappointed in God. The God he had trusted previously in his life seems to have failed to provide the grace Lewis had counted on being there. His disappointment is deep and painful, and he expresses it.

These are not the sorts of phrases we hear in weekly worship. But they are honest and heartfelt words that we may express in our own way. With the prophet Jeremiah, we trust God enough with our feelings that we can express anger and frustration over our loss and in our grief.

A relationship with God that does not move beyond anger and resentment is a relationship, but not one that opens us to grace. God desires an intimacy that flows from honesty and love.

We try to gather our thoughts and feelings when we are in this stage, although sometimes, as we have seen, a scream may be as appropriate as stringing words together. But when we are able to admit and express what is going on in our relationship with God, we will find our life with God has cleared up, rather like the world around us after a thunderstorm blows through. The cleanup can begin.

God is able to handle our anger. Just as we are able to speak clearly about anger with good friends, we can speak with God about our difficulties. God welcomes the faith and trust that we display when we speak of this anger, resentment, and disappointment we feel in our grief. We will welcome the relief that comes from a relationship that will continue and grow in this new soil that has been deepened and enriched by our honesty and trust in God.

To Think About

Has your willingness to express your anger toward God changed during your life? If so, how has it changed? If not, what is your reaction?

To Talk About

When you are feeling anger toward God, with a friend or counselor or clergyperson discuss that anger, your reasons for it, and possible ways you can work through it.

To Do

Write back to Jeremiah what you think God would have to say to him.

Prayer

I thank you, dear God, that your love for me is constant and not so much unchanging but willing to change to accommodate all the ways I can act, think, feel, and believe. Help me not to hide from you. Help me to come to you honestly. Help me to love you always, In Christ, amen.

STAGE EIGHT

We Resist Returning

THIRTY-SEVEN

To Remember, to Forget

Thus says the Lord,
> who makes a way in the sea,
> a path in the mighty waters,
who brings out chariot and horse,
> army and warrior;
they lie down, they cannot rise,
> they are extinguished, quenched like a wick:
Do not remember the former things,
> or consider the things of old.
I am about to do a new thing;
> now it springs forth, do you not perceive it?
> > —Isaiah 43:16–19

In 1389, an army of Ottoman Turks defeated a Serbian army in the Battle of Kosovo. Six hundred years later at a commemoration of the battle, Slobodan Milošević, a leader of Serbian forces in the bloody Balkan War, reiterated a cry many Serbs remember: "We shall not forget." That refusal to forget something that had happened six centuries before accounted for hundreds of thousands of deaths.

Not forgetting can be a virtue. Remembering your friends' anniversaries and favorite treats is kind and thoughtful. Remembering things that cause discomfort can also be important. Children learn to watch out for hot surfaces often through their own discomfort. But not forgetting can also lead to a refusal to move forward into a new situation.

Our human tendency is to try to hang on to what we have and where we are and who we are. Change can be unsettling and even frightening. We approach this stage of grief with the possibility of returning to a "normal" way of living, looking at life, and dealing with the day-to-day, ourselves, our neighbors, and our faith.

Why do we resist?

When we have suffered a loss, the world changes for us. Grief is a natural reaction in the process of living with that loss and change.

A significant reason for this resistance is that we either know or we intuit that what we are returning to is not what we left. We have changed in the course of our mourning. A significant presence in our previous life is no longer there. We have become familiar with grief and shock and depression and come through them as changed people.

The world around us is not the world we experienced before our loss. The people around us have changed; we see the world itself through changed eyes. We may have discarded activities and sites that were meaningful to us before the loss, and we may be exploring new practices and places.

Our relationship with God is not what it was. We have had sometimes harsh, sometimes painful conversations with God. We have looked at our value systems, made adjustments either intentionally or unintentionally. The God to whom we return will very likely not be the same "God" we knew previously. At least our concept and relationship to God most likely will have changed.

Such changes can be frightening and unappealing. Just staying where we are can sound attractive to us.

August 2013

(In Memory of Tom Barry, friend and sailor, Seattle)
So many boats sail today,
  Their captains watching
    Wind, wave, current, shore.

    Those on board trust the sailors' skill,
      Rest in the rhythm of the tides.
        They do not worry about day or destination.

      The same water is never the same,
        Is it, friend?
          Nor does the sailor never change.

      The sun rises and the day
        Is not created, but confirmed.
          Light shines on what is there.

        The sailor knows what he hopes
          And, when the voyage is over,
            The end, like the day, is confirmed.

          How many goodbyes can you say?
            Let grief carry you like a boat
              Under full sail, to deeper water.

The "new thing" God promises in Isaiah is always coming to us. We can find it difficult to welcome and may even resist receiving it. Relying on God's love and promises, though, we pray for the openness to embrace this new thing as we do God's many other gifts to us.

To Think About

Think about people you know who are very open to change. Think about those you know who resist change. What do you find appealing in each approach?

To Talk About

Have a conversation with a friend about what it was like to be away from home or some other familiar and comfortable place and then return to it. What feelings do you share? How do your feelings differ?

To Do

A novel written by Thomas Wolfe, late American author, is titled *You Can't Go Home Again*. Write a letter to him with your response to that idea.

Prayer

Gracious God, you are always doing a "new thing," and you are doing that not just to show off your power, not just for the sport of it, but because you know these new things free us to live and to move into the future with hope. Give me eyes to see what new things you are doing in my life. Help me greet them with faith and joy. In Christ, amen.

THIRTY-EIGHT

Who Am I? Returning and Yourself

To suffer a loss is to be changed. We are changed in our outer circumstances and inwardly. As we deal with our loss and grief and begin to think about returning to normal life, we may wonder whether we are ready for another change.

We wonder because the "normal" life we are returning to is not the same "normal" we experienced before our loss. In fact, no new day is a replica of the day before. The reality of loss and the changes we have lived through make that truth even more certain. It is no wonder, then, that we resist a return. We will find new patterns, new wisdom, and our new personal history make the world we reenter a different place for us.

Some of us can even grow used to mourning. We may experience satisfaction in people knowing we are sad. We may look into ourselves and desire a bit more sympathy.

Most of us are not the same "me" we were as we return to the flow of life. We have been through so much and likely have not yet processed everything about our experience. We may not have had the time or taken the time to look at how our minds and spirits have been rearranged. And even if we have been working hard to reflect on our experience and feel a deep measure of peace with ourselves, we may not be sure we want to take that "new me" into the world yet.

The German martyr to the Nazis, Pastor Dietrich Bonhoeffer, wrote this poem from his prison cell:

Who Am I?

Who am I? They often tell me
I stepped from my cell's confinement
Calmly, cheerfully, firmly,
Like a Squire from his country house.

Who am I? They often tell me
I used to speak to my warders
Freely and friendly and clearly,
As though it were mine to command.

Who am I? They also tell me
I bore the days of misfortune
Equably, smilingly, proudly,
like one accustomed to win.

Am I then really that which other men tell of?
Or am I only what I myself know of myself?
Restless and longing and sick, like a bird in a cage,
Struggling for breath, as though hands were compressing my throat,
Yearning for colors, for flowers, for the voices of birds,
Thirsting for words of kindness, for neighborliness,
Tossing in expectations of great events,
Powerlessly trembling for friends at an infinite distance,
Weary and empty at praying, at thinking, at making,
Faint, and ready to say farewell to it all.

Who am I? This or the Other?
Am I one person today and tomorrow another?
Am I both at once? A hypocrite before others,
And before myself a contemptible woebegone weakling?
Or is something within me still like a beaten army
Fleeing in disorder from victory already achieved?

Who am I? They mock me, these lonely questions of mine.
Whoever I am, Thou knowest, O God, I am thine![45]

The hope we are invited to hold on to as we resist a return is the same hope Bonhoeffer speaks to. Whoever we are, we are held by God.

To Think About

What changes in your life have made returning to "normal" more difficult and what changes in your life have made returning less difficult?

To Talk About

Have a conversation with a friend who has also suffered a loss. Share what about that loss made each of you more able to return to "normal" life. Were there things about each of your situations that made you less able to return?

To Do

Make a list of the activities you enjoy in what is a normal day for you.

Prayer

God, you are always calling me into a new day. Sometimes I am glad to follow, and I thank you for giving me that grace. Sometimes I am reluctant to respond. Help me to move into the future knowing that you will be with me there as you have always been with me. In Jesus's name, amen.

THIRTY-NINE

Go Home to Your Friends:
Returning and Others

Then people came to see what it was that had happened.
They came to Jesus and saw the demoniac sitting there,
clothed and in his right mind, the very man who had had
the legion; and they were afraid. Those who had seen what
had happened to the demoniac and to the swine reported
it. Then they began to beg Jesus to leave their neighborhood. As he was getting into the boat, the man who had
been possessed by demons begged him that he might be
with him. But Jesus refused, and said to him, "Go home to
your friends, and tell them how much the Lord has done
for you, and what mercy he has shown you."

—Mark 5:14–19

The loss and grief we have faced are certainly not to be
equated with the wild, violent life among the tombs
endured by a man possessed by a legion of demons.
Still, when we experience a loss and journey through
the phases of grief, our life among our own tombs can seem frightening to people.

Some people don't know how to communicate with us. They're afraid of saying the wrong thing. They might not know how to be with us without our loved one in the room—or now that we are unemployed or living in a temporary shelter while we wait for our home to be rebuilt.

We might feel reluctant to return to our relationships with others, perhaps because some of them have done or said things that hurt our feelings. They may not have meant to, but we remember the hurt feelings.

On the flip side, we may have taken out some of our sadness, pain, anger, or depression on other people. We may have been the ones who said hurtful things. We may have been the ones who didn't act "appropriately." Now that we realize what we've done, we may feel embarrassed or ashamed and resist returning to those relationships.

Change. Change happens in the course of our grief. How we see our own needs and gifts, how others see us, the value we put on relationships, and some relationships themselves may have changed. Some connections may not seem as important; some, more important. For sure, the relationships have been changed.

The good news is that God does not leave us wandering among the tombs. Jesus frees the man possessed by demons, and the people find him changed. The puzzling news—news we likely recognize from our own experience—is that others may resist seeing us as changed people.

The man himself resisted returning to his community. He wanted to become one of the traveling disciples and follow Jesus around Galilee, rather than remain in the village where he had experienced so much pain.

We also may want to remain where we are, apart from our old life. We might want to hold fast to the relative safety of our new life, one that is starting to feel familiar. We may wonder whether we want to reenter relationships that have changed, that might feel awkward, that we might have damaged when we have not been in our right minds, that might even harm and wound us.

But Jesus tells the man to go home to his friends.

That is good advice for us. It is good for us to know that such a return can be difficult—*and* that what we are experiencing is not unusual. But, in the end, it will be good for us to go home to our friends. As we return to the communities, our own presence may be a proclamation to others about how much God has done for us. We may also find the voice of God speaking to us from our newly appreciated and appreciative communities.

To Think About

In your current experience, do you find it difficult to return to a person or persons you had been with? What do you think might be the reasons? How could a return happen?

To Talk About

Have a conversation with a friend about the friendships you have had. Which ones have continued, and which ones have not? Talk with each other about why some continued and some didn't.

To Do

As you have been dealing with grief, has there ever been a time when you have taken out some of your difficult feelings on someone else? If there has been, write a note of apology to the person you may have hurt. If not, choose one of your friends who has been helpful during your grief and write a thank you note.

Prayer

Dear God, thank you for giving me a life that is richer in the textures of life and community, people and relationships than I am often aware of. Help me not to fear when people and circumstances change. Give me grace to enter again into the amazing flow of life. In Christ, amen.

For the Winter Is Now Past:
Returning and Creation

For now the winter is past,
    the rain is over and gone.
The flowers appear on the earth;
    the time of singing has come,
and the voice of the turtledove
    is heard in our land.
The fig tree puts forth its figs,
    and the vines are in blossom.

—Song of Songs 2:11–13

Coming through a journey of loss and grief is much like approaching the end of a winter. Whether that winter is one of blowing winds and blizzards or cool rains, when it ends most of us see the world coming back to life and life taking on a brighter color. But sometimes the effects of winter continue into spring. We need to make repairs following storms, pick up fallen branches, rake leaves and cut back perennials, replace storm windows with screens, or clean up messes the snow had hidden.

We might experience the closing of our grief journey in a similar way. We will likely encounter holdovers from the colder times. Those old snowdrifts can have an impact on our willingness to engage with the world, with creation.

Most likely, the places and things that helped us appreciate creation will not be the same for us. Certain meals, certain drinks, certain songs, certain places remind us of the pain we experienced. Something we loved, perhaps with another person, may bring reminders of our loss. A place we used to visit may be saying, "The loved one who came here with you will not come here again." That can be hard. We may wonder if we want to revisit these memories.

We will have changed through our grief. For most of us, how we think, how we feel, and how we perceive will be different. But when we let ourselves wonder whether what pleased us before our loss will continue to please or whether we will continue to enjoy what sustained us in our loss, we may be engaging in a second-guessing that will keep us from acting at all.

The only way we can figure out what will continue to give us joy is to try those things again. We visit those places, listen to that music, share those meals, look and listen and pay attention to the world outside and our own internal reactions.

The lovers in the Song of Song experience each other and the world with a sense of awe about the wonder of their relationship and the world around them. Bird song, scent of flowers, and fragrance of vine and fig add to the appreciation each one has of the self and the other. Creation is their partner—and ours—in relishing the fullness of God's grace and God's presence with each person.

Reluctance to return to a more active life in the world around us is understandable when we have felt the pain of loss in the

For the Winter Is Now Past: Returning and Creation

same world. But a return will also open the way to new meaning and meaningful encounters with the world around us.

To Think About

In your loss and grief, what places in your world do you not want to revisit? What about these places no longer pleases you? To what places would you like to return? What are the sounds, tastes, or scents you still enjoy?

To Talk About

Have a conversation with a friend about the things you like most in the world around you. If your friend talks about something you have not experienced but that attracts you, ask how to encounter that yourself.

To Do

Is there a place you used to love to go but have not visited for some time, perhaps because of a loss you have experienced? Make a specific plan to revisit that place.

Prayer

Dear God, open your world to me. Help me to see beauty and meaning around me. Help me to explore creation. Help me to find myself in the world around me. In Christ, amen.

An End to Childish Ways:
Returning and God

O Lord, you have searched me and known me.
You know when I sit down and when I rise up;
    you discern my thoughts from far away.
You search out my path and my lying down,
    and are acquainted with all my ways.
Even before a word is on my tongue,
    O Lord, you know it completely.
You hem me in, behind and before,
    and lay your hand upon me.
Such knowledge is too wonderful for me;
    it is so high that I cannot attain it.

—Psalm 139:1–6

Many of us have shared something very personal and meaningful with someone and then later thought we said more than we intended or felt comfortable with. Sometimes when we do that we wonder what our next encounter with the friend will be, and we may be a little shy or reluctant to begin a new conversation with that person.

An End to Childish Ways: Returning and God

In our grief, as people of faith we have quite likely said things to God that we had not before. We may have questioned God's love or very existence. We may have been angry with God, accused God of being cruel or uncaring. We probably have gone to God with tears and groans.

As we include God in our grief, we may have found, with the psalmist, that God knows us better than we know ourselves, that God has "searched" and "known" us. God's searching and deep knowledge of us and our own questioning and self-revealing can make us feel exposed and vulnerable—the way we feel with a friend to whom we might have revealed, we later think, too much.

When we are moving to a new place in our grief, we may wonder about our relationship with God. That relationship has changed. Perhaps our very concept of God has been challenged, explored, adjusted. We might wonder whether God is truly trustworthy. Or our relationship may have deepened beyond our earlier understanding of who God is and how God relates to us.

Ideally, we find when we are grieving that vulnerability is not a bad thing, that it opens us to ourselves, to others, and to God. The apostle Paul writes, "When I was a child, I spoke like a child, I thought like a child, I reasoned like a child; when I became an adult, I put an end to childish ways" (1 Corinthians 13:11). In our grief, we may find ourselves moving beyond an earlier, simpler, and maybe "childish" concept of God to a more mature relationship. We may come to know God not simply as distant and judgmental. God is not a cosmic Santa Claus or problem fixer for the deserving but a parent to us. God is companion with us all through our lives, one who laughs with us, grieves with us, and always enters each new day with us.

So, reluctance to return to our relationship with God can be a quite natural part of the grieving process. We have changed.

"God" has changed in our understanding of who God is. Our lives have changed, and we try to move into relationships not fearful of that change but anticipating where it will lead us. We are not completely certain about the future, but we are confident that God will be an intimate part of it.

To Think About

As you look back over your life and the ways you thought of God, try to think of images that might represent how you thought of God at each stage. Which of those images do you still find appropriate for you? Which of those have you left behind or now find do not fit?

To Talk About

We all have images of who God is for us. Explore with a friend the understanding each of you has of who God is. Do not argue or correct but listen and learn.

To Do

Write a dialogue between yourself and God (yes, you may speak for God here!). Talk about what you are thinking and feeling and see how God responds to you.

Prayer

God, we have been through a lot, haven't we? Help me to realize that we have been through life together. Help me to feel and to find comfort and joy in your presence. Hold me, dear God. Amen.

STAGE NINE

Gradually Hope Comes Through

FORTY-TWO

Something Quite Unexpected

Something quite unexpected has happened. It came this morning early. For various reasons, not in themselves at all mysterious, my heart was lighter than it had been for weeks. And suddenly at the very moment when, so far, I mourned H. least, I remembered her best. Indeed it was something (almost) better than memory; an instantaneous unanswerable impression. To say it was like a meeting would be going too far. Yet there was that in it which tempts one to use those words. It was as if the lifting of the sorrow removed a barrier.[46]

—C. S. Lewis, *A Grief Observed*

C. S. Lewis, who wrote *A Grief Observed* as a way of living through his grief and mourning at the death of his wife, notes the unexpected but much-appreciated appearance of healing and hope. We may experience this as well, a welcome greeting from healing and hope. At some point as we process our grief, we may feel like we are finally coming home after a long and trying journey and begin to sense some hope.

Hope for what? Hope for a lessening of the grief but not of the memory. Hope for the return of some kind of normal rhythm, even when we may have been reluctant to enter it. Hope to move again into new relationships, perhaps new loves and new friendships. Hope that it is not wishful thinking but a quiet assurance that God, indeed, does love us.

We hope the future is open for us, not tied to the past, to our loss and grief, but not forgetting that past and the places or persons we are grieving. When we can think of the future and feel anticipation rather than anxiety, we know that hope is coming through.

People who grieve understand that the journey is not a straight line. The process will backtrack or stall or move more slowly and sometimes more quickly than we might anticipate or appreciate.

Hope sometimes shines through for a bit and then seems to move away or disappear for a while. Hope will appear more clearly at some points and seem more distant at others. When that happens, don't despair but understand that this is part of the process.

What is important for us, though, is that we have seen hope. We know that hope, as an open future, as new relationships, as a healing of our souls, and as a renewed relationship with God's love, is coming. We have seen it and we will see it again.

I believe that I shall see the goodness of the Lord
    in the land of the living.
Wait for the Lord;
    be strong, and let your heart take courage;
    wait for the Lord!
—Psalm 27:13–14

Something Quite Unexpected

When I was young, my father worked at a bakery in our hometown. My dad was an especial favorite of the various dogs that lived in our house. He loved them, fed them, talked to them—he was much more than the family alpha dog. With their acute ears, they could hear his Buick (always a Buick) coming a block away. They would rise, tails wagging, and head to the back door where my dad would soon enter. The dogs, his wife, and his children were all happy at his return.

Our hope is something like that. We have had a vision of what it looks like and we anticipate that vision becoming a reality for us. We wait for it, as the psalmist waits for the Lord, knowing we will see the goodness of God in the land of the living.

To Think About

Throughout your life, you have experienced hope in different situations and forms. Take time for quiet thought and remember how you experienced hope as a young person and since then.

To Talk About

Have a conversation with a friend about how each of you defines *hope* and how each of you has experienced hope throughout your lives. Talk about the similarities and the peculiarities of each person's definition and experiences.

To Do

Make a list of five reasons you have hope for the future.

Prayer

God of hope, you have been my partner all through my years. I thank you because your presence has given me strength and peace. I ask you to be with me as I move into the future. I don't know what it will be or bring, but I trust that you will be with me. Continue to hold me, in Jesus's name, amen.

The Blue Water Ahead:
Hope and Yourself

And you, child, will be called the prophet of the Most High;
    for you will go before the Lord to prepare his ways,
to give knowledge of salvation to his people
    by the forgiveness of their sins.
By the tender mercy of our God,
    the dawn from on high will break upon us,
to give light to those who sit in darkness and in the
shadow of death,
    to guide our feet into the way of peace.

—Luke 1:76–79

Paulson Lake is in the Boundary Waters Canoe Area Wilderness of far northern Minnesota. It is a small lake but perhaps one of the most beautiful. It is crystal clear, clean and cold, surrounded by high hills. To reach the lake, canoeists paddle through a series of lakes connected by portages—paths (often rocky) over which canoeists must carrying everything—canoes, food and tents, rain gear and extra clothes, fishing rods—all the heavy gear that makes a canoe trip possible.

A particular attraction for canoeists is the route to and from Paulson Lake. Approaching from the south, several short portages climb up and down sharp ridges. To the north, a two-mile-long portage goes up and down hills, through swamps and around windfalls.

As canoeists approach the northern end of that portage, they can see the blue waters of enormous Seagull Lake through the trees. The agony of the portage is nearly forgotten, and it is not unusual for those carrying canoes and gear packs to walk right into the sandy-bottomed lake and exult in the cool, waist-deep water.

Carrying packs and canoes across a two-mile portage has much in common with moving through loss and grief. When hope comes through, it is like the sun shining off a lake at the end of a portage. We have a sense that we will soon set aside the burdens we have been carrying. There will be time to cool off, rest, relax, and regain strength.

Canoeing is also different from grief in significant ways. Some canoeists regularly go out of their way to visit Paulson Lake. Besides its beauty, the satisfaction of finishing the long portage compels them. Unlike canoeists who map out their trip, though, those of us who grieve do not choose our losses. We do not choose to enter grief. It comes to us. We may not have the opportunity to prepare for it, the way one might prepare for a portage or a race. We find ourselves in it.

Sometimes on a portage, we can see the next lake from a ridge, but then we descend back into a dark valley or an inky swamp before we see the blue promise again. And so hope comes to us but sometimes recedes again before it returns. Still, even before we reach the end, we know we have come through. We are nearing the end of this journey. It will always be a part of who we are, but

The Blue Water Ahead: Hope and Yourself

we move forward knowing that we are capable and that we have resources for the days ahead.

Those resources probably include the love of family and friends who have helped us reach a point where we can see hope. They include wise words, welcome writings, places of rest and reflection—signs that God has been with us through the loss and the grief.

We see ourselves differently when we come to this place in our grief journey. As Zechariah sings in the Bible passage that begins this devotion, we can become "prophets of the most high," that is, people who point to what is holy and hopeful. The tender mercy of God comes like hope, light comes to us even as we have become familiar with the darkness and shadow of death.

We will, more and more, find ourselves moving in the way of peace. We will find ourselves living peacefully and hopefully.

To Think About

As you look back over the journey you are still on, having faced loss and experienced grief, think about times when you saw hope for yourself. What brought that hope about? How did you feel at those times?

To Talk About

Have a conversation with someone who has also had experience with loss and grief. Talk together about how you each experienced hope. How did it appear? What people and places were involved? Talk about how that experience and hope have changed each of you.

To Do

Imagine hope as a living person. Write a letter to hope about how it has been a part of your journey and what parts it has played. What advice do you want to offer hope? If you feel like it, thank hope.

Prayer

God of peace, I thank you for the gifts of hope and peace. Grant me the grace to receive and experience them both. Give me the grace to share that hope and peace with brothers and sisters who need them. I ask this in Jesus's name, amen.

FORTY-FOUR

Friendships—New and Renewed: Hope and Others

Above all, maintain constant love for one another, for love covers a multitude of sins. Be hospitable to one another without complaining. Like good stewards of the manifold grace of God, serve one another with whatever gift each of you has received. Whoever speaks must do so as one speaking the very words of God; whoever serves must do so with the strength that God supplies, so that God may be glorified in all things through Jesus Christ. To him belong the glory and the power forever and ever. Amen.

—1 Peter 4:8–11

Granger Westberg quotes from Rabbi Joshua Liebman's book *Peace of Mind* as he encourages us to find community:

The melody that the loved one played upon the piano of your life will never be played quite that way again, but we must not close the keyboard and allow the instrument to gather dust. We must seek out other artists of the spirit, new friends who gradually will help us to find the road to life again, who will walk that road with us.[47]

When we begin to see hope, we find ourselves more open to community. We feel the burden of our loss and grief becoming less and our willingness to be with others growing. Our time with others is both a sign of the emerging hope and a means for that hope to increase.

We will find value in our relationships with others. Self-assurance will come with renewed friendships and new friendships. We will find ourselves more willing to share with others both the struggles and the wisdom we have experienced in our journey through grief. We will hear and learn from others about their own journeys.

Beyond that deeper sharing, simply being in community is a valuable opportunity to experience again the variety of human experience. We will know again that we can laugh and be playful. We will find we enjoy conversations, shared meals, walks with friends, or simply quietly being together.

The apostle Peter writes about the gifts of community. Hospitality, service, love for others, and our willingness to speak as God gives us the ability are all signs of God's presence and love. God is glorified in such community, and we, too, as part of those communities, are edified. We learn (or learn again) that life can be good.

A gift of our humanity is to share with each other and to both bear the burdens of others and, sometimes, simply to bear *with* others. Our exercise of patience is a gift—a gift to us from others who have walked through our grief with us, and a gift we give them as hope begins to come through for us.

In the give and take of community, we will find other "artists of the spirit," as Rabbi Liebman describes those who will walk with us. They will help us to see the world with fresh eyes and renewed hope. They will color the world, describe our lives as a meaningful poem or a beautiful piece of music. They will provide a strong frame around the portrait of our new lives. An artist friend of mine expressed the view that graphic art helps people see what isn't there and written art helps them see what is there that they may not have noticed. Both are movements into clearer vision and a greater appreciation of the world.

To Think About

Who are the old friends to whom you have returned or to whom you would enjoy returning? Who are the new friends you have made or would like to make as you move through loss and grief?

To Talk About

Have a conversation with a friend about experiences each of you has had with other people that helped you feel more hopeful. Your experiences may have involved time with a team or a neighborhood, a workplace, or an opportunity to share a hobby. Explore together why this was the case.

To Do

When you are ready, choose a social or community gathering you would like to be part of. If you are not ready, make a list of four events or opportunities you would like to be part of and set a date to attend or participate in one.

Prayer

Gracious God, I thank you for the people in my life. I thank you especially for those who have helped me through my grief. And I thank you for those people who have helped me to hope for my future. I especially remember these friends. Thank you for them. In Christ, amen.

FORTY-FIVE

All Nature Sings:
Hope and Creation

This is my Father's world, and to my listening ears
all nature sings and round me rings the music of the spheres.
This is my Father's world; I rest me in the thought
of Rocks and trees, of skies and seas; his hand the
  wonders wrought.[48]

Whether the name we use for God is Father or Mother, we believe that God's parental love and care is shown not only in and through us but also in the world God has given into our care and continues to create. The words of the hymn "This Is My Father's World" reflect this belief and assure us that the hymn writer has found peace and wonder in the world around.

When hope begins to come through, our relationships not only with ourselves and others but also with the wider world take on new significance. We begin, perhaps once again, to see ourselves as part of the world around us, and the time we spend outside our homes or classrooms or offices can become more healing and enjoyable.

When we are first suffering a loss and the shock that follows, it is difficult for us to focus on much other than our feelings. That, of course, is natural. As we move through our grief we can begin to look around us. One of the things we will see in the hope that gradually returns is the earth around us—nature, of course, but also our town's parks and streets, the yards and gardens we mow and tend and appreciate as they perfume our lives, the roads we travel to new places, adventures, people, challenges, and satisfactions. All these are part of creation, and we see them differently through hopeful eyes.

Hoping in Mid-November

I hope warm weather stays around
at least for a while
and that the winter provides the snow we need
and no more
and that I continue to feel good
and that my family is healthy and happy
and that my siblings are healthy and happy
and that my in-laws are healthy and happy
and that people learn to forgive
and that people learn to love
and that people learn to heal
and that people learn
and that dahlias are perennials.

We can look around us and see the world where weather, our health, our family and friends, the ways people behave, and, of course, the beauty of perennials help us to be thankful we are in such a world. We raise our eyes and our hearts and find the world opening again to us and for us. When the world is an open place, the world welcomes us home and we feel, once again, at home in our world.

We may have had more time to live in the world, in creation, before a loss made our lives painful. We may not have realized at the time that we were experiencing creation as a partner and a participant. But that is what we were doing. As hope begins to be a part of our lives, we will find a new or renewed interest and involvement in the world around us. We will be able to take time to be in nature, to listen, to watch, and to let the world around us speak to us. In the voice of the world, we can also hear the voice of God who is mother and father and sibling and friend and Christ, who in his humanity is also and always part of creation.

To Think About

In the poem above, the poet hopes "that dahlias are perennials." What hopes do you have about the world around you? Why do you have these hopes? To maintain beauty, to serve creation, to help the environment, or some other reason?

To Talk About

If you are able to walk, take a stroll or hike with another person through a park or rural or wilderness area. Talk to each other about what you are seeing and feeling because of your surroundings. If you are unable to walk, take a drive with a friend or look for opportunities that organizations in your community might offer to spend time out in the country and talk about those same things.

To Do

Take time to find a quiet place outside to sit and listen. A day later write about your time there—either in a poem, a short essay, or a letter to yourself.

Prayer

God, creator of everything in the universe, I am awestruck at your creation. But my awe becomes comfort and peace when I remember that you are also creating me. Thank you for your love, your concern, and your molding of me throughout my life. Continue to open me to your presence with me. In Jesus's name, amen.

FORTY-SIX

Simple Things:
Hope and God

When he was at the table with them, he took bread, blessed and broke it, and gave it to them. Then their eyes were opened, and they recognized him; and he vanished from their sight. They said to each other, "Were not our hearts burning within us while he was talking to us on the road, while he was opening the scriptures to us?"

—Luke 24:30–32

Two disciples are walking toward the village of Emmaus. This is Easter Sunday. Jesus appears next to them and asks what they are talking about, and they express surprise he hasn't heard about the prophet from Nazareth. "We had hoped he would be the one to redeem Israel," they say. They had heard rumors of the resurrection but weren't sure what to think or believe. Jesus speaks to them of "the things about himself in all the scriptures," but their eyes aren't open until he breaks bread with them.

They found their hope had been granted, though not in the way they had expected.

God comes to us most often in simple things. When hope begins to return to us in our grief journey, we rarely experience an earth-shattering event that removes all doubt and sorrow and replaces them with pure faith and joy. Rather, we become aware of the presence of the Creator in the ordinary. We meet God in a sunrise or sunset, in the rich variety of the world around us, in the goodness of human love and relationships, and in shared meals with loved ones. That breaking of the bread can whisper something of God's presence.

Even as God moves in and settles with us in the ordinary, we encounter God in the places where God has promised to be present. Worshiping with our faith community, receiving the holy bread and wine, may, without our anticipating it, move us more deeply than it has in the past. A woman attending Easter worship after the death of her husband hears the pastor, speaking of Mary Magdalene, say, "Maybe only those who have experienced grief can see angels," and the grace and mercy of God gently warm her.

As with our other relationships, our relationship with God has changed in the course of our loss and grief. We may give up our assumptions about a God who is all sunshine and happiness, and encounter a God who knows mangers and tombs, life and death—a God who gladly meets us at our best and at our worst and continues to love us.

Sometimes we will feel absolutely certain of God's presence and love. And sometimes we will again wonder if we can count on God. We have experienced that doubt in the past, and it will continue to be part of our faith walk. We don't panic or despair when those times arrive. We know they will not last. We ask ourselves what, if anything, may have brought that on and we claim God's promise that, as we have experienced in the past, the faith that is a nestling faith will again be ours.

In the ordinary and the sacred, hope gradually enters our lives, our daily experiences, and blesses our ordinariness. We hear a word that tells us the future that had seemed closed and distant now is open and promising and comes to us in many ways. We discover that God has not been absent and now returned, but that the God who is abounding in steadfast love has been with us through our grieving and will walk with us into the future.

To Think About

Looking back over your life, when has it been easy to hope in God? When has such hope been more difficult? Ask yourself what might be the reasons for each experience.

To Talk About

"Maybe only those who have experienced grief can see angels." Share that sentence with a friend and discuss what it means and whether you agree with it. What do you each think *angels* might be?

To Do

Read the twenty-fourth chapter of Luke. Then put yourself in the scene as the third disciple on the road. Write down what you would have said in the conversation and what you might have felt at the breaking of the bread.

Prayer

God of hope and life, Jesus, you who love me, you met the disciples on the road to Emmaus and did not end but blessed their journey. You have been with me. You are giving me hope for my future. Continue to walk with me; continue to bless my future, I ask you, amen.

STAGE TEN

We Struggle to
Affirm Reality

FORTY-SEVEN

Not as Those Who Have
No Hope

> Now concerning love of the brothers and sisters, you do
> not need to have anyone write to you, for you yourselves
> have been taught by God to love one another. . . . But we
> do not want you to be uninformed, brothers and sisters,
> about those who have died, so that you may not grieve
> as others do who have no hope. For since we believe that
> Jesus died and rose again, even so, through Jesus, God
> will bring with him those who have died.
>
> —1 Thessalonians 4:9–14

Granger Westberg notes many times in his book, but
especially in his summary of stage ten, that a mature
and practiced faith is essential for us as we are moving
through grief and, of course, moving through our lives.
A mature faith is not based on simply reciting creeds or prin-
ciples and agreeing with what they say. While statements of faith
are important, faith is a relationship with God. Paul writes to the
Thessalonians about their love for their brothers and sisters but

also their love for outsiders. This, like all of our relationships, is connected to God's love for them and their love for and their faith in God.

Faith, our relationship with God, can be a relationship that wrestles. It contends now and then, it asks questions, it wonders why and how and is not afraid, like the writers of the Bible, to challenge God.

Faith can also be a relationship that nestles. Like a child or a young bird, it finds comfort simply in resting in God, in being comforted and nourished by God. I once was a guest preacher at a church in a small town in Wisconsin. Behind the altar was a gold-tinted window in the shape of a cross. As I began the sermon, I looked through the window and saw a bird's nest and the mother feeding the nestlings. Spontaneously, I suggested to the congregation, "You can listen to the sermon or watch the window behind me. That may tell you as much about God."

Neither a wrestling faith nor a nestling faith is the right one. Both are important parts of our relationship with God. Sometimes, as we discover in our grief work, it is necessary and helpful to argue with God, to wrestle with the doubts and questions and anger that we feel at our loss. Sometimes, as we also discover, it is necessary and helpful and comforting to nestle in God, to rest, to be nurtured, to weep and to be cared for.

We are encouraged by Scripture to "not grieve as others do who have no hope" (1 Thess 4:13). Grief is natural and good. But Paul advises that we grieve as people who have hope because God has come to us in God's grace. Sometimes we wrestle with that grace and sometimes we nestle in it, but in all times, God is at work in us. We are at work, like athletes or apprentices learning to master a new trade, becoming people of faith and hope.

The time, reflection, conversation, and prayer we have given to our grief are exercises of faith. These exercises mature and prepare us to affirm life. They have taught us how we are connected to others, to the world, and to God. A loss has an impact on all relationships, and the restoration of hope also impacts and strengthens our relationships.

And as Westberg points out, to affirm is to pronounce something good.[49] We are affirming even the struggles and pain we have lived, pronouncing them good, and are now moving into the relationships made possible by the honest struggles of our journey.

To Think About

In your own journey through loss and grief, when have you found you have a wrestling faith and when a nestling faith? As you look at these times, what do you think are the benefits of a faith relationship that wrestles and one that nestles?

To Talk About

Have a conversation with a friend about times when you were experiencing a change and easily affirmed the new reality and times when affirming the new thing you were experiencing was more difficult.

To Do

The apostle Paul wrote, "But we do not want you to be uninformed, brothers and sisters, about those who have died, so that you may not grieve as others do who have no hope." Rewrite these words in a way that reflects your own grief journey.

Prayer

Dear God, give me faith and hope so that whether I am wrestling with you or nestling in you, I might always find joy and peace in your presence. In Jesus's name, amen.

FORTY-EIGHT

A New Home:
Reality and Yourself

Now the Lord said to Abram, "Go from your country
and your kindred and your father's house to the land that
I will show you. I will make of you a great nation, and I
will bless you, and make your name great, so that you will
be a blessing."

—Genesis 12:1–2

The Bible includes many stories about people on the
move. Some movements are grand, like the Israelites'
exodus from Egypt, but most take place on a smaller
scale. Abram is told to leave what is familiar and go to
a land he has yet to see. There, he is promised, he will produce a
great nation. And so, Abram moves to a new home.

The struggle to affirm the reality we enter as people who have
lived through grief is like moving into a new place. Much is familiar, but much can seem strange. We are still the people we were,
and we have changed and been changed.

As I was writing these meditations I was in the process of
moving to a different home in a different city and state. When

that move was nearly complete (and those of us who have moved into new homes know something of that process!), I found myself feeling both the same and different, both familiar and alien, even to myself.

Kitchens are kitchens, but this new one doesn't have exactly the same layout. I find some things where I expect to find them; other things I have to hunt for. The cups are in a different place, the spices aren't arranged just the same, and the neighbors are new. I have to learn to use an electric stove after years of cooking with natural gas. But I will learn this new house and community, and it will become a home.

When we live through a loss and the grief that ensues, in most ways we are still the same person we were. But we are moving from one home to another. As we live through our own shock and emotion, depression and distress, panic and guilt, anger and resistance, we learn about ourselves, our strong walls as well as our cracks and chinks, many the same as before. But we also discover some parts of ourselves have been repaired, others built anew. Yet we settle in, learn to live within the house that we are, and give thanks for the blessings of this new place, until we come to see the future with hope.

People in some Christian traditions ask blessings on their homes on January 6, the Epiphany. "May Christ bless this home," reads one Latin prayer for the occasion. As we move into a new home as selves that are the same and yet different, we can as well ask this blessing on ourselves and our homes:

January 6

Christus Mansionem Benedicat
May this home be blessed
With love that blossoms as hope.

May this home be blessed
With healing that may not cure
And lives not shackled by fear.

May this home be blessed
With faith that is quiet trust.
May this home be blessed,
Be a Sacrament of love
And a place of welcome peace.

May this home be blessed
By the One who is promise
May this home be blessed
By the One who is presence
By the One who is Blessing.

May this home be blessed.

To Think About

What is the layout of the new house and new home you now are? What do you find familiar and what do you find different? Think about how you are adjusting to this new you.

To Talk About

Have a conversation with a friend about what it was like, for them and for you, to move into a new house, apartment, or community. How did each of you settle in? Talk about how this is like the personal changes you each have experienced this past year.

To Do

Write down five things you look forward to doing or seeing or experiencing in the next year. Make plans to carry them out.

Prayer

Gracious and generous God, you are always inviting us into new life. Help me to enter the newness I see in myself with a sense of gratitude to you and hope for myself. I ask this in Jesus's name, amen.

FORTY-NINE

People Who Need People: Reality and Others

When [Jesus] returned to Capernaum after some days, it was reported that he was at home. So many gathered around that there was no longer room for them, not even in front of the door; and he was speaking the word to them. Then some people came, bringing to him a paralyzed man, carried by four of them. And when they could not bring him to Jesus because of the crowd, they removed the roof above him; and after having dug through it, they let down the mat on which the paralytic lay. When Jesus saw their faith, he said to the paralytic, "Son, your sins are forgiven. . . . I say to you, stand up, take your mat and go to your home." And he stood up, and immediately took the mat and went out before all of them; so that they were all amazed and glorified God, saying, "We have never seen anything like this!"

—Mark 2:1–5, 11–12

In the course of moving through the stages of grief, one of the important things we realize is how much we need other people. We may be grieving the loss of one we loved; that alone tells us how significant other people are for us. But we also have found that the presence or kindness or meaningful words of people we know and people we have come to know have brought healing to us.

In the story of Jesus healing the man with paralysis, the friends carry their friend. They bear his burden. More than anything else, they want to bring him to this one who they have heard can heal. The crowd of people who don't know their friend won't stop them. The roof of Jesus's home won't stop them. They dig through the roof and lower their friend, laying him at Jesus's feet.

We have had friends like that. They may not have carried our mats, but they shared our burdens. The probably didn't dig through a roof, but they helped us move through obstacles to our own healing, through our shock or depression or anger or resentments, our physical pain, our resistance—all our natural processes of grief. Friends, counselors, medical people, or clergypersons have helped us realize the challenges we have been experiencing are not abnormal but also aren't permanent.

As we move through the process of grief, some of the relationships we counted on will end. We also enter a new reality with these friends and helpers. Our developing relationships, especially with family and friends, will no longer be primarily those of helped and helpers. These were necessary roles for us, but they are changing.

We had the blessing of loved ones and friends who shared our burdens. We had the blessing of those who helped us chop through our own restricting ceilings. Now we have the blessing of relationships built on shared experiences, shared interests, and shared lives.

As we affirm the reality that our new selves are "good," we also affirm that our community of family, friends, and acquaintances—gifts from God—are "good." We and our friends have been deepened and strengthened by traveling through hard times together. Now we may also be able to enjoy more good times together.

Some of us may feel strange returning to activities with others that involve fun and pleasure and happiness. This return to enjoying life, like all that we have experienced through our loss and grief, is natural. We play games; we attend contests; we share a festive meal; we go to a play or a movie; we go camping or boating or just have a quiet time together of conversation and snacks.

We do what or whom we are mourning no favors by denying ourselves the pleasures of life. We may struggle with that return to "normal" and affirming that new reality. We have, like the man in the parable, laid on mats of our own as we journey through grief. We are invited and enabled also to pick them up and go home.

To Think About

What activities with other people did you enjoy in the past? Are you ready to return to them? What new activities are you ready to try?

To Talk About

If there are people nearby with whom you have enjoyed time together in social settings, meet with them and share some of your memories of those times. Share what plans each of you have for the future.

To Do

What new activities would you like to try out with other people? Make a list of them. Prioritize the list and make plans to try them out.

Prayer

Gracious God, I thank you for my family and friends. I thank you for those who have been a part of my life for a long time. I thank you also for new friends. I thank you for those people you sent to help me in my grief. Bless me and bless my loved ones, in Jesus's name, amen.

FIFTY

A Renewed World:
Reality and Creation

And, when you watch the rainbow,
See how the earth is greener
And birds sing just a little sweeter song.
See how the plants are growing,
See how the streams are flowing
Because the clouds and rain have come and gone.
Let our love be just the same
As that good life-giving rain
And the cooling summer clouds.
So, when we're through on earth
There may be just a bit more mirth
Because of the love we gave to each other.

—Brent D. Christianson

I wrote the words above as part of a song for my wife. The earth itself can both reflect something of our feelings and moods and, when we listen, can even communicate with us as we express the emotions we are feeling. We have likely experienced that connection in the past, and we will experience it in the future. We are part of and partners with creation, and it shares in our experience of life.

We have had times when the world around us seemed to match perfectly just what we were feeling—a foggy day when we were pensive, a sunny day when we were joyful, a cold rainy day when we were feeling a bit down. We have also experienced times when the world around us insisted on being itself without checking our moods. But in all those experiences, we encountered something of our intimate connection to the world around us.

When we are dealing with loss and grief, we can have difficulty being attuned to the world around us. The "world" inside us can have plenty of its own storms or fog or frigid temperatures or too-hot days. But now, having been gardeners in our interior landscape, we are beginning again to look around us. We will try to affirm the grace of creation. We will try to echo God's word that every aspect of creation is good.

As we move to a new place in our lives, having learned about ourselves and our ability to live through difficult times, we emerge as renewed people. We will once again be able to pay attention to the world around us, whether the natural world of creation or the built creation of our towns and cities, our homes and neighborhoods, our work and play.

We may revisit a place that was significant for another relationship and encounter happy thoughts of those days. Or we may find the return is a painful reminder of the loss we have grieved and have difficulty allowing ourselves to affirm this new reality. In good times and bad, though, we keep in mind that even a thunderstorm can be a witness to love and community.

We are not returning to things just like they were, but we are turning to a renewed world. This renewed world will offer some of the pleasures and challenges we experienced in the past. But there will be new pleasures and new challenges that we, renewed ourselves, will live in and through.

To Think About

Are there places in your world that you associate with the loss you have grieved? Which ones are you reluctant to return to and why? Which ones would you like to return to and why?

To Talk About

The portion of the song that begins this meditation reflects on the world after a rain storm. Have a conversation with a friend about your memories of a weather event that left an impression on you and your world. What made it significant?

To Do

If you have been reluctant to pay attention to creation, choose one place you think of as welcoming and make a plan to visit it. If you have been reentering creation easily, make a plan to explore a favorite place with a good friend.

Prayer

God, thank you for this world. It is an amazing place that sometimes thrills me and sometimes frightens me, but I know I am a part of it. Thank you for your constant creation, so powerful and sometimes frightening, but that also refreshes and renews all things. In Jesus's name, amen.

FIFTY-ONE

The Day the Lord Has Made:
Reality and God

O give thanks to the Lord, for he is good;
    his steadfast love endures forever!
. . . .
Out of my distress I called on the Lord;
    the Lord answered me and set me in a broad place.
With the Lord on my side I do not fear.
    What can mortals do to me?
. . . .
I thank you that you have answered me
    and have become my salvation.
The stone that the builders rejected
    has become the chief cornerstone.
This is the Lord's doing;
    it is marvelous in our eyes.
This is the day that the Lord has made;
    let us rejoice and be glad in it.

—Psalm 118:1–24

The Day the Lord Has Made: Reality and God

The airplane had encountered fairly severe turbulence. Nobody got sick, but nobody was feeling exactly well. The seatbelt signs were on almost continually. The attendants were not able to serve food or drink. A lot of people were praying; some were crying. The pilot announced preparations for landing, the plane descended, the airport and runway came in view, the wheels met the tarmac, and the plane slowed to approach the gate.

Everyone cheered. They thanked the attendants, they shouted gratitude to the pilot as they deplaned. They hugged each other, and they looked forward to seeing those who were waiting for them with even more enthusiasm than they had at the flight's beginning.

When we live through a loss and the following grief, the experience can sometimes feel as uncertain or turbulent as an uncomfortable flight. When we find ourselves safely at the end of that phase of our journey and ready for more to come, we feel gratitude.

We feel gratitude for the inner strength we found. We feel gratitude for the people who were with us, helping us through the hard times. We feel thankful for the world that has nourished and sustained us. We feel grateful to the God who has been with us from the beginning of our lives, through the loss we sustained and the grief we experienced, and who now meets us at the gate.

We approach the final stage of our living through loss and grief as changed people. Necessarily, our relationship with God, our concept of just who God is, and our feelings about God have gone through many changes, too. This happens in any relationship, even in the best of times. And in close relationships, that ebb and flow is especially important and healing. God is not different, but our relationship, our understanding, and our gratitude have all taken a different and, we hope, a renewed form.

We seek to affirm the goodness of this relationship. We look at God and we can hear the psalmist saying God is good and God's steadfast love endures forever. Forever is great, but we are grateful that God's steadfast love is with us for our moments in this forever. We give thanks that we are able at last to enter a new day affirming the Lord has made this day, and we rejoice and are glad in it.

To Think About

Think about times when you have been moved to thank God. Remember the circumstances and the reasons for your thanksgiving.

To Talk About

Have a conversation with a friend or a counselor or your clergy-person about how you have seen God's presence in your loss and grief. What were some of your feelings during this time? Has your relationship with God changed at all? If so, how?

To Do

Write a list of seven things to thank God for. Offer a prayer of thanksgiving for one each day of the next week.

Prayer

Dear God, you have given me all I am and all I have. I thank you for such steadfast love and generous mercy. Today I am especially thankful for _____. Come with me now. Walk with me into the future that you have opened for me. In Christ, amen.

FIFTY-TWO

Grief and Hope

Talking to Grief

Ah, Grief, I should not treat you
like a homeless dog
who comes to the back door
for a crust, for a meatless bone.
I should trust you.

I should coax you
into the house and give you
your own corner,
a worn mat to lie on,
your own water dish.

You think I don't know you've been living
under my porch.
You long for your real place to be readied
before winter comes. You need
your name,
your collar and tag. You need
the right to warn off intruders,
to consider

my house your own
and me your person
and yourself
my own dog.

—Denise Levertov[50]

For the fifty-two weeks we have been living through our loss and the grief it brought about, we have acknowledged it was there, "invited it into our home," and learned to live with it. Denise Levertov imagines grief as a dog that needs a home and the griever as the one who takes it in.

For Levertov, unrecognized grief wanders about outside, tipping over the garbage, rifling through our yard and our possessions, and leaving us worse off than we were before. When we recognize and accept that grief, acknowledge its flow, that homeless dog becomes a part of our home, no longer strange and dangerous but a kind of domesticated companion as we move forward.

We are at the end of these devotions, but we recognize that there really are no endings in life. All of them are the beginning of other journeys. Even death, for people of faith, is not an end but a beginning of a new reality for us. We do not mourn as people who have no faith, but we mourn as people whose faith allows us to feel deeply, to be honest about our emotions, willing to explore our lives, and able to move beyond grief and into hope.

Hope, after we have encountered the shadows of life, is not wishful thinking about what we want. Hope comes about as we live honestly and directly. We take the world as we find it but do not let the world alone dictate who we are or how we are. Grace allows us to see the faults and fractures in ourselves and our world and yet continue to see even more the presence of the God who has strengthened and guided us.

We have become familiar with our losses and our grief. We have a sense of our strengths and our growth areas. We have experienced the joy of friendships with others, the beauty and variety of the world around us, and the God who assures us of divine presence and grace that lasts a lifetime and beyond.

We find ourselves a new creation, able to move into the coming days with confidence. We give thanks for relationships renewed and new relationships that we will continue to enjoy. We discover that God, whose love and presence have been with us even during our days and nights of doubt and anger, continues to love us and be present with us and will go with us in an ever-renewing relationship of faith.

We move into hope with that experience and those assurances. We know we are different people than we were, seasoned and experienced. We have experienced the help of friends and family. We are able to enjoy this world into which God has placed us. This world has been a place where we have suffered and grieved. This world has been the place where God has met us in our grief and, with all God's gifts of community and creation and our own selves, blessed us and strengthened us. We move ahead in hope and confidence that God, who walks with us, will continue to bless and strengthen us.

To Think About

How have you changed in your encounter with loss and grief? What words would you use to describe yourself today compared with fifty-two weeks ago?

To Talk About

Have a conversation with someone you know to have also made a journey through grief. Read Denise Levertov's poem together and talk about the image she uses. What other images capture your experience of grief?

To Do

You know and will continue to encounter people who have suffered a loss and are dealing with their grief. You have likely been made stronger and more empathetic from your own experience. Share yourself. Reach out to one person. Let them know you are willing to listen and be with them.

Prayer

Gracious God, healer and friend, thank you for loving me. Thank you for being with me. Thank you for moving ahead with me. In Jesus's name, amen.

Notes

1. Unless otherwise noted, all poems are my own compositions.
2. Granger E. Westberg, *Good Grief* (Minneapolis: Fortress Press, 2018), 13.
3. Westberg, *Good Grief*, 14.
4. John Updike, "Ode to Healing," *Facing Nature: Poems* (New York: Alfred A. Knopf, 1985), 84.
5. Westberg, *Good Grief*, 14–15.
6. C. S. Lewis, *A Grief Observed* (New York: HarperOne, 1996), 11.
7. Westberg *Good Grief*, 15.
8. Stephen Dunn, "Ars Poetica," in *Loosestrife: Poems* (New York: W. W. Norton, 1998), 32.
9. Folliott S. Pierpoint, "For the Beauty of the Earth," *Evangelical Lutheran Worship* (Minneapolis: Augsburg Fortress, 2006), hymn 879.
10. Marty Haugen, "O God, Why Are You Silent?," in *Evangelical Lutheran Worship* (Minneapolis: Augsburg Fortress, 2006), hymn 703.
11. Westberg, *Good Grief*, 21.
12. Rolf Jacobsen, "Sunflower," in *The Winged Energy of Delight: Selected Translations*, ed. and trans. Robert Bly (New York: HarperCollins, 2004), 196.
13. Lewis, *A Grief Observed*, 30.
14. Lewis, *A Grief Observed*, 10.

15. Henri Nouwen, *The Wounded Healer: Ministry in Contemporary Society* (New York: Doubleday, 1979).
16. Chana Bloch, "The Potato Eaters," in *Swimming in the Rain: New and Selected Poems, 1980–2015* (Pittsburgh: Autumn House, 2015).
17. Robert Bly, "A Gathering of Men with Robert Bly," BillMoyers.com, transcript, January 8, 1990, https://tinyurl.com/yc7t4etc.
18. Paul Verlaine, "Il pleure dans mon coeur," in *Romances sans paroles*, 1874, Poetica.fr, https://tinyurl.com/yclhbduj, my translation.
19. Lewis, *A Grief Observed*, 29.
20. Anne Lamott, *Help, Thanks, Wow: The Three Essential Prayers* (New York: Riverhead, 2012).
21. Westberg, *Good Grief*, 29.
22. Martin Luther, *Luther's Works*, vol. 54, *Table Talk* (Philadelphia: Fortress Press, 1967), 18.
23. Lewis, *A Grief Observed*, 3.
24. Alden Nowlan, "Bobby Sands," in *What Happened When He Went to the Store for Bread* (Minneapolis: Thousands Press, 2000), 150.
25. Westberg, *Good Grief*, 32.
26. Thomas A. Dorsey, "Precious Lord, Take My Hand," in *Evangelical Lutheran Worship* (Minneapolis: Augsburg Fortress, 2006), hymn 773.
27. Westberg, *Good Grief*, 38–42.
28. Johnny Nash, "I Can See Clearly Now," track 7 on *I Can See Clearly Now*, Epic Records, 1972.
29. Wendell Berry, *The Selected Poems of Wendell Berry* (Berkeley, CA: Counterpoint, 1998), 30.
30. Qing Li, *Forest Bathing: How Trees Can Help You Find Health and Happiness* (New York: Viking, 2018).
31. Westberg, *Good Grief*, 48.
32. Westberg, *Good Grief*, 48–49.
33. Westberg, *Good Grief*, 48.

34. Martin Luther, *Luther's Works*, vol. 34, *Word and Sacrament*, vol. 1, ed. Jaroslav Pelikan (St. Louis: Concordia, 1972), 264.
35. Westberg, *Good Grief*, 49.
36. Westberg, *Good Grief*, 49.
37. Daniel D. Stuhlman, "The Story of Two Brothers—Revisited," *Kol Safran*, May 30, 2012, https://tinyurl.com/yakdvo36.
38. Westberg, *Good Grief*, 55–57.
39. Mary Lavin, *The Story of the Widow's Son* (Mankato, MN: Creative Education, 1993).
40. *Broadway Danny Rose*, directed by Woody Allen (1984), quoted in Sander H. Lee, *Woody Allen's Angst: Philosophical Commentaries on His Serious Films* (Jefferson, NC: McFarland, 2013), 167.
41. Martin Luther, *Luther's Works*, vol. 1, *Lectures on Genesis: Chapters 1–5*, ed. Jaroslav Pelikan (St. Louis: Concordia, 1958), 174.
42. Lewis, *A Grief Observed*, 29.
43. Westberg, *Good Grief*, 63.
44. Westberg, *Good Grief*, 64.
45. Dietrich Bonhoeffer, *Letters and Papers from Prison*, ed. Eberhard Bethge (New York: Touchstone, 1997), 347.
46. Lewis, *A Grief Observed*, 44–45.
47. Joshua Loth Liebman, *Peace of Mind* (London: William Heinemann, 1946), 114, quoted in Westberg, *Good Grief*, 79.
48. Malthie Babcock, "This Is My Father's World," in *Evangelical Lutheran Worship* (Minneapolis: Augsburg Fortress, 2006), hymn 824.
49. Westberg, *Good Grief*, 86.
50. Denise Levertov, *Selected Poems*, ed. Paul A. Lacey (New York: New Directions, 2003), 120.